Strategies *for* Success

By James M. Dornan

Strategies
for
Success

NETWORK TwentyOne
Global Business Support Systems
EUROPE • AMERICAS • AFRICA • PACIFIC RIM

Table of Contents

FOREWORD

The moment that I met Jim and Nancy Dornan, I knew they were winners. They're incredible people with great hearts and wonderful personalities. More importantly, they have a clear vision for their lives. And a huge part of that vision focuses on helping people.

As Jim and I got to know each other, I quickly realized that we had discovered many of the same truths in life, truths that you learn when you're a leader. Jim understands success, personal growth, and leadership in a way that few people do. And that insight has helped him build one of the most effective business organizations in the world.

The key to Jim and Nancy's success has been personal development - first of themselves and then of the people around them. They hope to continue that process with you through *Strategies for Success*. It is an excellent blue-print for your personal growth, because it takes thirty years of experience and insights, and distills them into one easy-to-read volume. From it, you will learn how to become a positive thinker who deals with stress and failure effectively. You'll develop a vision for your life, set goals, and manage your time better. And you'll sharpen your leadership and communication skills. By the time you're done, you'll be ready to go to a whole new level!

Do you want to be successful? Then turn the page and keep reading. If you put the ideas in the next ten chapters into practice, your success is almost inevitable. And once the process begins, then it's your turn to find people to help become a success too.

John Maxwell
Atlanta, Georgia

INTRODUCTION

I still remember the first time I came in contact with the world of self-improvement. I was a young engineer at McDonnell Douglas in Long Beach, California, and I was given a copy of *The Magic of Thinking Big* by David Schwartz. I had tackled the challenges of an Aeronautical and Astronautical Engineering degree from Purdue University, and was well equipped for a career in engineering—at least that's what I thought. Yet after only a short few months into my career I began to sense that I had missed something. Technical know-how would provide me a decent job for 40 years, but it became obvious that true success was more elusive; most of us had a strategy for a job but nothing close to a dependable strategy for success.

I remember feeling out of control of my own future. Advanced degrees, technical or even superior competence and long work hours were often rewarded, ultimately, with dead-end positions, frustration, layoffs, and a general sense of insecurity or dissatisfaction for those who once had such clear hopes and dreams. Obviously something was missing, something that would either improve one's chances of ultimate success or at least lead to a more stress-free life.

The Magic of Thinking Big was such a simple book, certainly no match for *Theory of Aeroelasticity* of Quantum Physics, and yet it was profound in its simplicity. The realization that one's *attitude* and *thinking* were equal to or even more significant than one's knowledge was a new concept to me.

Now, that was more than 25 years ago and there were very few books of that type around. Napoleon Hill's *Think and Grow Rich* or Norman Vincent Peale's *Power of Positive Thinking* were two classics, as well as Dale Carnegie's *How to Win Friends and Influence People.* For some reason, my engineering mind immediately grasped the logic of these principles and I was forever changed. It wasn't technical or even scientific in the usual sense, but these simple principles of goal-setting, self-talk and attitude were indeed a key to a successful life, even in a technical field.

Today self improvement has become a huge industry, with great writers and observers like Dennis Waitley, Zig Ziglar, Stephen

Covey, John Maxwell, and others too numerous to mention. For a quarter century I have studied nearly all of these authors and some have even become friends. I have read hundreds of books on these subjects, but more importantly I have tried to apply them. Whether I was trying to succeed as a father or husband or as a student or leader, I needed to grow and change as a person to move to the next level of life.

My passion for the value of these principles came as a result of much study, followed by much activity, followed by much failure and disappointment, followed by persistence and eventually success in the same degree.

Raising three children, especially in the teenage years, 29 years of marriage to a dynamo named Nancy, the birth and life-deepening challenges of our son, Eric, who has undergone 30 brain surgeries as a result of Spina Bifida and currently blesses my life from the unique vantage point of his power wheel chair, and the building from scratch of a group of companies with offices now in 18 countries has taught me many lessons. Lord willing, I anticipate many more lessons in the future.

My business gives me the unique opportunity to travel the world and meet with literally thousands of people who are sincerely seeking a strategy for success. They are sometimes professionals, such as doctors or attorneys, sometimes clerical or service people, business owners or executives and even students. But they all want to know what it takes to live a successful life or to be a successful leader and influence others.

My business often takes me to remote and unusual places. I work regularly with people in Hungary, Poland and throughout Eastern Europe. I have significant involvement in Turkey, Greece, Indonesia, the Philippines, South America and even China. Many of these cultures have had little exposure to these concepts and are far behind in their understanding of them.

In my travels I am regularly asked to summarize the principles I have lived and learned about for so long. This book is simply an attempt to condense some of the important areas to give anyone who is serious about true success a foundation upon which to build. My hope is that these simple truths will help you develop your own strategy for success.

J.D.

8

-chapter one-

The Successful Person Practices ...
POSITIVE THINKING

*Attitude is the first quality that marks the successful man.
If he has a positive attitude and is a positive thinker who likes
challenges and difficult situations, then he has half his
success achieved.*
                                              —*Lowell Peacock*

*There is little difference in people, but that little difference
makes a big difference. The little difference is attitude. The big
difference is whether it is positive or negative.*

                                              —*Clement Stone*

YOUR ATTITUDE DETERMINES YOUR ALTITUDE
The difference between those who are successful and those
who are unsuccessful in life is this: the lives of those who are successful are governed and controlled by the thoughts of their best
hour, their greatest optimism and their most triumphant experience. Unsuccessful people, on the other hand, are guided and controlled by their past failures and doubt. That means you are only an
attitude away from success!

*You are only an attitude away
from success!*

Some people will try to tell you that others have made them
who they are, or that circumstances dictate their place in life. They
even say that they can't help how they feel. But it's not what's
around us that makes us who we are. In the end, we are the only
ones responsible for the way we look at life. As Viktor Frankl, sur-

9

vivor of a prison camp in Nazi Germany said, "The last of the human freedoms is to choose one's attitude in any given set of circumstances."

Maltbie D. Babcock said, "One of the most common mistakes and one of the costliest is thinking that success is due to some genius, some magic, something or other which we do not possess." Success really is determined by something within your control. It is a result of your attitude. How high you will fly is limited more by how you think than by any other factor..

Our attitudes determine a great deal of what happens to us.

1. *Our attitude toward life will determine life's attitude toward us.*
2. *Our attitude toward others will determine their attitude toward us.*
3. *Our attitude at the beginning of a task will determine the success of its outcome more than anything else.*
4. *The higher you go in any organization of value, the better attitude you'll find.*

No wonder it has been said that we create our own environment— mental, emotional, physical, spiritual—by the attitudes we develop.

I have never seen a consistently successful person with a bad attitude.

Having a positive attitude does not guarantee success, although it does improve your day-to-day life. However, if you have a negative attitude, you cannot be successful. I have never seen a consistently successful person with a bad attitude.

THE NEGATIVE EFFECTS OF A NEGATIVE ATTITUDE

You are where you are and what you are because of the dominating thoughts that occupy your mind. I heard the story of a man who swallowed an entire raw egg, shell and all. He was afraid to move for fear it would break, yet afraid to sit still for fear it would hatch. Like him, a negative person is trapped by his thoughts and the circumstances they create.

Here are six possible results of continual negative thinking:

1. NEGATIVE THINKING CLOUDS CRITICAL DECISION TIMES

When a person always looks for and finds the negative things in life, he begins a habit that's hard to overcome. He will see every situation as a series of obstacles. Thus, even when a positive opportunity presents itself, the negative person can't see it and will never seize it.

So what's the difference between an obstacle and an opportunity anyway? Our attitude toward it. Abraham Lincoln, considered by many to be the greatest president in the history of the United States, said, "Success is going from failure to failure without losing your enthusiasm."

Instead of seeking the negative, refuse to accept it until you have thoroughly explored the positive. You'll be cultivating a habit of positive thinking, which will make it easier for you to make clear decisions at critical decision times.

2. NEGATIVE THINKING IS CONTAGIOUS

I'm sure you've heard the old saying, "Birds of a feather flock together." It's really true, even more with people than with animals. The animals who flock together are already alike, but humans will actually change and become like one another by spending time together.

You've probably noticed that people who have been married a long time start to act alike, and some even begin to look alike. Old friends do the same. And this is never more true than in the area of the attitude. If you spend long periods of time with people who think negatively, you will begin to take on their attitude. Being exposed to negative people is like being exposed to radiation. You can survive low doses for brief periods of time, but continuous exposure can kill you.

3. NEGATIVE THINKING BLOWS EVERYTHING OUT OF PERSPECTIVE

You've probably been around people who blow everything out of proportion. When there's a leak in the roof, they treat it like a hurricane. All they see in life is doom and gloom. These are people who consider "Murphy's Law" their life motto: "Nothing is as *easy* as it looks; everything takes *longer* than you expect; and if anything can go *wrong*, it will and at the *worst* possible moment."

To counter that kind of thinking, I look at life according to a law that my friend John Maxwell came up with. Maxwell's Law goes like this: "Nothing is as *hard* as it looks; everything is *more rewarding* than you expect; and if anything can go *right*, it will and at the *best* possible moment."

The most harmful result of Murphy's Law-thinking is that it distorts every situation. Successful people constantly base their decisions on an accurate perspective. This helps them to see opportunities for what they really are and make sound decisions. One big obstacle to that kind of success is a skewed and negative perspective.

Maxwell's Law:
Nothing is as hard *as it looks;*
everything is more *rewarding*
than you expect;
and if anything can go right, *it will,*
and at the best *possible moment.*

---

4. NEGATIVE THINKING DECREASES HOPE
Where there is no hope in the future, there is no power in the present. Negative thinking destroys faith and undermines hope over the long run. It slowly but continually demoralizes us, destroying our momentum.

5. NEGATIVE THINKING LIMITS OUR POTENTIAL
People cannot continually behave in a manner that is inconsistent with the way they see themselves. Negative people think the worst, not only of the world around them, but also of themselves. Because of this, they expect little and often receive less. You've probably heard some of these responses when new ideas are introduced:

12

"It will never work;"
"We've never done it that way before;"
"We're doing fine without it;"
"We can't afford it;"
"We're not ready for it;"
"It's not our responsibility."
That's negative thinking at work, placing limitations on success and drawing boundaries where none exist.

King Solomon, often referred to as the wisest ruler in the world, said in Proverbs 23:7 of the Bible: "As a man thinketh in his heart, so is he." In other words, people become what they believe. We cannot achieve what we do not aim for. And we won't aim for anything that we've convinced ourselves that we can never achieve. When a negative thinker has low expectations of himself, he clamps a lid on his ability to achieve. This makes him his own worst enemy.

6. NEGATIVE THINKING KEEPS US FROM ENJOYING LIFE

Negative thinkers spend the entire voyage of life hanging over the rail, seasick. Regardless of present circumstances, they find something to be disappointed about. Many have adopted Chisolm's Law: "Anytime things appear to be getting better, you have overlooked something."

For negative people, the glass is never half full; it is always half empty. They expect-and thus receive-the worst in life. They remind me of the young mountain climber who was traveling with an experienced guide high in the mountains. Early one cold, snowy morning, the young climber was suddenly jolted awake by a tremendous "BOOM!" He thought the world was coming to an end. But when he cried out in fear, the guide calmly said, "What you hear is the ice cracking as the sun hits it. It's not the end of the world-just the dawning of a new day."

If we are to live life to its fullest and reach our potential, we must see the circumstances of life in a positive light-as the dawn of a new day.

THE POWER OF POSITIVE THINKING

Alfred A. Montapert said, "The environment you fashion out of your thoughts ... your beliefs ... your ideals ... your philosophy ... is the only climate you will ever live in." If you think positively, then your environment will be positive. What an incredible idea! Positive thinking has amazing powers, even over circumstances.

Robert J. Hastings said, "Places and circumstances never guarantee happiness. You must decide within yourself whether you want to be happy. And once you've decided, happiness comes much easier."

You might believe that some people are born thinking positively and others negatively, and that we're stuck with whatever disposition we get. But while it's true that we are born with the *inclination* to be one way or the other, we *can* overcome that inclination. The bottom line is that positive thinking can be learned by anyone, regardless of circumstances, temperament, or intellect.

> *The bottom line is that positive thinking*
> *can be learned by anyone,*
> *regardless of circumstances,*
> *temperament, or intellect.*

Let me give you ten principles that can help you cultivate or improve your ability to think positively:

1. ACT, WALK, TALK, AND THINK
AS YOU WISH TO BECOME

Most people wait until they *feel* positive before they do things positively. But they have things backwards, and that handicaps them. Attitude actually *follows* action. When we take positive steps, this leads to positive thoughts. And positive thoughts lead to a positive attitude. The best way to begin overcoming a negative mindset is to move in a positive direction.

2. CULTIVATE SUCCESSFUL, POSITIVE THOUGHTS
IN YOUR MIND

Multimillionaire U.S. industrialist Andrew Carnegie said, "The man who acquires the ability to take full possession of his own mind may take possession of anything else to which he is justly entitled." When we begin to *think* in positive terms, and we see our-selves as successful, we start to become successful.

---

*Give your thoughts
to what's positive
and successful.
Don't feed the weeds.*

To harvest the fruit of a successful life, think of yourself as a farmer. We cannot simply plant a few positive seeds, and then walk away. Instead, we must continually water those seeds, then nurture and fertilize the plants as they grow. If we neglect to give them our attention, weeds of negative thinking will spring up, rob the soil of its nutrients, and choke the positive plants until they die.

Don't let this happen to your crop! Give your thoughts to what's positive and successful. Don't feed the weeds. As it says in Philippians 4:8 of the Bible, "Whatsoever things are true, whatsoever things are honest, whatsoever things are just, whatsoever things are pure, whatsoever things are lovely, whatsoever things are of good report . . . think on these things." Choose daily to focus on the positive.

3. RADIATE THE ATTITUDE OF WELL-BEING, CONFIDENCE, AND PURPOSE

By thinking and acting in a positive manner, you will begin to develop a sense of well-being. Your confidence will increase, and you'll get a stronger sense of purpose in your life. Then, because everyone enjoys being with positive people, others will become more attracted to you.

As you radiate a positive outlook, you'll have more opportuni-ties to develop positive relationships. Use those connections to help those around you to become more positive.

4. TREAT EVERYONE YOU MEET AS THE MOST IMPORTANT PERSON ON EARTH

We live in a fast-paced world. Most of us move quickly from place to place focused on what we need to get accomplished. As a result, we often neglect to make time for the people we encounter during the day.

If you take time with the people you meet and give them your full attention in a positive way, it will make their day. The positive and considerate act will add value to them. And their response will be to add value to you.

5. MAKE EVERY PERSON YOU MEET FEEL NEEDED, IMPORTANT, AND APPRECIATED

All people have the desire to feel important. It is at the core of who we are as human beings. So when you meet that need in people, it makes them feel positive about themselves and you, creating a win-win situation. As nineteenth century American philosopher-poet Ralph Waldo Emerson said, "It is one of the most beautiful compensations of this life that no man can sincerely try to help another without helping himself."

Another benefit of making others feel important is that they will respond in kind. The treatment we receive is often a reflection of how we treat others. It's like what I heard about two different men who were moving to a new town. As the first man reached the outskirts of town, he stopped at a gas station and asked the attendant who worked there, "How are the people here?"

Before replying, the attendant asked, "Well, how were the people in the last town where you lived?"

The first man scowled, "They were really awful and unfriendly."

At this, the attendant paused a moment, then gave his answer: "People are just the same in this town."

Later that day, the second man drove into the same gas station and asked the attendant the same question: "How are the people in this town?"

Once again, the attendant asked, "Well, how were the people in the last town where you lived?"

This man smiled in memory, and replied, "Oh they were wonderful. They were really friendly!"

This time, without hesitation, the attendant answered, "You'll find that the people in this town are exactly the same."

That gas station attendant knew that the attitude you bring with you is the attitude you will get from others.

16

6. LOOK FOR THE BEST IN EVERYONE

I believe there is good in the worst of us and bad in the best of us. What you look for is what you see, so it's important to look for the best.

I've been blessed with wonderful family, friends, and colleagues. In part, that has been a gift from God. But it is also a result of my positive expectations for those around me. I make a habit of mentally placing a "10" on the heads of everyone I meet. In other words, if we evaluate people on a scale of 1 to 10 (10 being the highest), we should expect everyone to perform and act like a "10," and really believe it. More often than not, people rise to our positive expectations.

Looking for the best in others also makes them feel good about themselves. It helps them to grow and strive to be the best they can be. And it creates a positive environment.

7. DON'T TALK ABOUT YOUR HEALTH
UNLESS IT IS GOOD

Few things in life give people negative feelings faster than a person who talks all the time about his poor health. The first time or two that it happens, people will be sympathetic. After that, they will become irritated and negative. Eventually, they will avoid the person altogether. Share negative news about your health only with your closest friends and family.

8. LOOK EVERYWHERE FOR THE BEST IN NEW IDEAS

Positive thinkers are constantly looking for great new ideas, because new ideas can increase our potential for success. As French author Victor Hugo said, "There's nothing more powerful than an idea whose time has come."

Some people believe that great ideas come only to the geniuses of the world. But finding great ideas is more a function of attitude than aptitude. An open-minded, creative person looks for ideas anywhere he can find them. And he is slow to reject any idea until he has examined it thoroughly for any good it might contain. It is said that Thomas Edison, one of the world's greatest inventors, discovered some of his greatest inventions when he examined an invention that had gone wrong and discovered another unintended use for it.

17

9. AVOID PETTINESS

Positive thinkers don't expend time and energy on petty things because pettiness can sidetrack them from their goals and priorities. We should strive to react in proportion to the actual situation. Pettiness occurs when we react too strongly—disproportionately more than the situation requires. Consider these outrageous reactions to petty situations:

A Chinese emperor once went to war over the breaking of a teapot.

Sweden and Poland fought in 1654 because the King of Sweden discovered that his name in an official dispatch was followed by only two etceteras, while the King of Poland's dispatch had three.

About 900 years ago, a dispute between Modena and Bologna over a well bucket began a war which devastated Europe.

The spilling of a glass of water over the Marquis de Torey led to war between France and England.

A small boy, by throwing a pebble at the Duc de Gruise, led to the massacre of Vassy and the Thirty Years' War.

Although it's unlikely that any of us will start a war because of personal pettiness, we can certainly make ourselves and others around us unhappy because of it. Just remember, a person is only as big as the things that make him angry.

10. DEVELOP A SPIRIT OF GIVING

Albert Schweitzer, physician and missionary to Africa, said, "The purpose of human life is to serve and to show compassion and the will to help others." The most positive contribution a positive thinker can make is through giving to others.

*How can a person resist someone
who is trying to help him
solve a problem?*

Harry Bullis, former chairman of the board of General Mills, used to give his salesmen the following advice: "Forget about the sales you hope to make and concentrate on the service you want to render." He knew that the moment our attention is centered on services to others, we become more dynamic, more forceful and harder to resist. After all, how can a person resist someone who is trying to help him solve a problem?

"I tell our salesmen," said Bullis, "that if they would start out each morning with the thought, 'I want to help as many people as possible today,' instead of, 'I want to make as many sales as possible today,' they would find a more easy and open approach to their buyers and they would make more sales. He who goes out to help his fellow man to a happier and easier way of life is exercising the highest type salesmanship."

As giving to others becomes a way of life, it's impossible to anticipate the positive results it can bring. It reminds me of the a story I once heard about a man named Sadhu Sundar Singh. One day he and a companion were traveling through a mountain pass high in the Himalayas. Rounding a corner, they suddenly came across a man lying motionless in the snow. Sundar Singh wanted to stop and help the unfortunate man, but his companion refused, saying, "We shall lose our lives if we burden ourselves with him."

But Sundar Singh would not think of leaving the unconscious man to die in the ice and snow, so he stayed behind. After his companion bade him farewell and moved on, Sundar Singh lifted the poor traveler onto his back and slowly bore the man onward. After about an hour, the heat from Sundar Singh's body began to warm the poor frozen fellow, and he awoke. Soon the man could walk, and they began hiking together side by side. After crossing another ridge, they caught up with Singh's former companion. Unfortunately, they found him dead—frozen by the cold.

Sundar Singh was willing to give all that he had—even his life—for another person. In the process he found life. In contrast, his callous companion sought to save his life, and ended up losing it.

THE FRUIT OF POSITIVE THINKING— POSITIVE LIVING

Positive thinking can change your life. It can put you into the position to succeed in any venture you desire to pursue. Here are just a few of its results. There are more, but these alone could be enough to put you on the road to success:

SELF CONFIDENCE

When you are a positive thinker, you believe in yourself and others. So you become more willing to try new things, to take more chances. And as a result, you achieve more.

Thinking positively enables you to maximize your potential. As time goes by, you understand better what you can and cannot do, which makes you more secure. Eventually, even failures can't erode your self confidence. You know that those mistakes don't change who you are, and you believe that things will turn out for the best in the long run.

INITIATIVE

People who believe that life is negative tend to do nothing and hope that the bad things won't happen to them. But when you're positive, you can't wait to try new experiences and make good things happen. A willingness to believe that life is positive can motivate you to try new things.

PERSISTENCE

When you believe that positive things will happen for you, you're more willing to keep going until those positive things occur. Even in the face of setbacks, positive thinkers are persistent. They see setbacks as temporary, and know that quitting is usually a permanent solution to a temporary problem.

*Quitting is a permanent solution
to a temporary problem.*

CREATIVITY

Albert Einstein said, "In my experience, the best creative work is never done when one is unhappy." That's a great insight from one of the most creative thinkers of our century. A focus on the positive promotes greater willingness to explore, question, and seek new answers. That's because when you're positive, the world is filled with unlimited possibilities. Or as Pogo, the positive cartoon possum drawn by the late Walt Kelly, once said, "We are confronted with insurmountable opportunities."

LEADERSHIP

Learning to become a great leader is a life-long process, but it begins with your relationships with others. And people will not follow someone they don't like—not for long anyway. And rarely do people genuinely like negative people.

The French General Napoleon Bonaparte once said, "A leader is a dealer in hope." In spite of his other faults, he understood that leaders instill in their people a hope for success and a belief in themselves. And positive leaders empower people to accomplish their goals.

GROWTH

A positive attitude can open many doors, including the opportunity for growth. That's because the right attitude makes you hungry for growth, and continual growth is one of the most common characteristics of successful people.

THE ABILITY TO PRODUCE RESULTS

W. W. Ziege said, "Nothing can stop the man with the right mental attitude from achieving his goal; nothing on earth can help the man with the wrong mental attitude." Positive thinking helps you to produce results, because it puts you in a position to act rather than react. This means you can set and work toward worthwhile goals that lead to success, rather than fighting your way out of negative situations every day.

Where success is concerned, people are not measured in inches, or pounds, or college degrees, or family background. They are measured by the size of their thinking, because how big we think determines the size of our accomplishments.

How big we think is determined by the way we think. And the way we think is one of the few things in life that we can control. As someone once said, "We cannot direct the wind . . . but we can adjust the sails."

We cannot direct the wind . . .
but we can adjust the sails.

21

Never underestimate the power of your thinking. My friend John Maxwell has written this about *Attitude:*

It is the "advance man" of our true selves.
Its roots are inward but its fruit is outward.
It is our best friend or our worst enemy.
It is more honest and more consistent than our words.
It is an outward look based on past experiences.
It is a thing which draws people to us or repels them.
It is never content until it is expressed.
It is the librarian of our past.
It is the speaker of our present.
It is the prophet of our future.

Having a positive attitude may not guarantee success. But it can put you on the road that leads to success. Then whether or not you arrive there will be determined by what you do along the way.

SUCCESS STRATEGY ACTIVITIES

Try to incorporate as many of these activities into your life as possible. You may want to keep a journal or chart to keep track of your progress. Remember that becoming a positive thinker is an ongoing process. If you are able consistently to perform these activities for a year, you will find that your outlook and quality of life have improved tremendously.

1. Pick a positive quote each week (you can start by using some of the quotes in this chapter) and write it down on a 3 X 5 card. Carry the card with you every day that week. Read and think about the quote periodically throughout the day. Put it where you will see it frequently during the day, such as on your desk, the dashboard of your car, or your bathroom mirror. Consciously make each quote a part of your thinking for that week.

2. Pick a person in your life about whom you ordinarily think negative thoughts. Determine to look for positive qualities in that person and to replace your negative thoughts with those positive ones. If you believe in God, also pray for that person, asking God to bless him or her.

3. One day a week, have a "10-day." Get up in the morning and decide that you will see everyone you meet as a "10." Then treat them as "10s." You'll be amazed at the responses you get from people who you have been overlooking or underestimating. Many of your relationships will improve as a result.

4. Designate one day a week as "positive thinking day." Eliminate the words "can't," "never," and "won't" from your vocabulary the entire day. At times when you might otherwise say, "It won't work," "We've never done it that way before," or "I can't do that," ask yourself what can be done. Look for hidden possibilities and opportunities in everything you do throughout the day.

5. At least once a week, find an opportunity to give to others. Do something special for your spouse or children. Help a neighbor or co-worker. Do a small kindness for a stranger. And if you can give to someone else anonymously, that's even better. You will be doubly blessed.

———

-chapter two-

The Successful Person Knows How to . . .
OVERCOME FAILURE

Failure isn't failure unless you don't learn from it.

—Dr. Ronald Niednagel

Ninety percent of all those who fail are not actually defeated....They simply quit.

—Paul J. Meyer

One of the most critical factors determining a person's success is how he or she deals with failure. Anyone who desires to be successful must develop strategies to overcome and keep going forward. Without those strategies, failure can lead to discouragement, which can lead to defeat.

FEAR OF FAILURE

Failure. Even the sound of the word is negative. What other word—except "death"—instills such fear in people? When you hear someone say that a person is a failure, you might conjure up quite a mental image—someone living in poverty or friendless, devoid of success, a positive future, or even hope.

People fear failure for many reasons. Here are a few:

FEAR OF CRITICISM

It's incredible how much some people worry about criticism. It's almost as though they live by a statement made sarcastically by Jan Spoelman: "If in doubt, take it personally."

Most of the great achievers in history were bitterly criticized, yet chose to persevere. One of my favorite examples is eighteenth century British evangelist George Whitefield. He was vilified probably more than any other figure of his era. His enemies

24

Most of the great achievers in history were bitterly criticized, yet chose to persevere.

threatened to murder him, then hired men to do the job. They excommunicated him and ordered him out of town, but he refused to go. They locked him out of their churches and forced him to preach in the streets. They hired buffoons to dress like the devil and mock him. They pelted him with dirt, eggs, tomatoes, and pieces of dead cat. More than once they hurled rocks at him until his head was covered with blood.

Some of the greatest people of Whitefield's time—Dr. Samuel Johnson, Sir Joshua Reynolds, Oliver Goldsmith, William Hogarth, Horace Walpole, the Duchess of Buckingham—heaped their scorn on him.

But he continued on with his mission despite their criticism and opposition. Thousands of people came to the fields outside of London to listen to him. He preached to the coal miners in Wales and Scotland. And he successfully raised money for orphanages, and went on to lead the "Great Awakening" in America.

Whitefield probably experienced ten "failures" before he went to sleep each night, and faced even greater criticism every day, but he didn't give up. Because he knew in his heart that what he was doing was right, he continued.

If you tend to fear criticism, stay focused on what you know is right, and spend less time worrying about what others think of you. Some people will always have something negative to say. Take heart from this statement by Lloyd Cory: "It's 100 times easier to criticize than to create."

FEAR OF TAKING A RISK

Walt Disney, a great visionary and one of the most creative men of the twentieth century, said, "All our dreams can come true—if we have the courage to pursue them." Think about that: If every person

Go out on a limb—after all, that's where the fruit is.

25

who ever had a great idea had the courage to act on it, the world would be very different. Unfortunately, few of us overcome the fear associated with risk, and we never move forward.

In order to be successful, you have to take chances. Go out on a limb—after all, that's where the fruit is.

FEAR OF LOSING SELF-CONFIDENCE

Norman Vincent Peale said, "Believe you are defeated, believe it long enough, and it is likely to become a fact." Some people fear failure because they believe it will cause them to lose self confidence. As a result, they try to put themselves into positions where they can't fail. Unfortunately, those positions also keep them from achieving anything out of the ordinary. By "playing it safe," they consign themselves to a life of mediocrity. Ironically, that doesn't help their self-confidence much. Instead, any confidence they might have had will be plagued with doubts about what might have been possible.

If you're going to risk losing your self-confidence anyway, why not do it trying to achieve your very best? If you try and fail, you've lost nothing. If you try and achieve any success at all, you're better off. On the other hand, if you try nothing, *you will never have any chance at success.*

FEAR OF NEVER GETTING A SECOND CHANCE

This is one of the greatest reasons for fearing failure. Many people believe that they have only one chance at success. They think that if they fail, they've lost that chance forever. Amazingly, if those people only knew how many famous, successful people failed their first time out, it would give them renewed hope.

Henry Ford said, "Failure is only the opportunity to begin again more intelligently." And Ford certainly knew about failure firsthand. In his first two attempts in the auto industry, his companies went bankrupt and failed. But his third try succeeded: Today, the Ford Motor Company is still going strong; it's one of the largest automobile manufacturers in the world.

Another famous "failure" was a young man whose life dream was to attend the United States Military Academy at West Point and then to serve his country. But when he applied to West Point, he was turned down—twice. After his third application, he was finally accepted. That young man's name? Douglas MacArthur.

MacArthur eventually became one of the highest-ranking generals in the United States, and served as commander in chief of the Allied forces in the Pacific during World War II. Like Henry Ford, he failed not once, but twice, in pursuit of his dream. But also like Ford, he never gave up. As a result, he finally succeeded.

> *Forget spending time and energy*
> *trying to avoid failure;*
> *instead focus on dealing with it*
> *in a successful way.*

No one avoids failure. That may sound incredibly simple, but it's true. We will all fail at some time in life. When we realize that it's impossible to completely avoid failure, we're free to take risks. Forget spending time and energy trying to avoid failure; instead, focus on dealing with it in a successful way.

Many good-hearted, intelligent, hard-working people have let failure get the better of them. They see it as something final. So when they hit obstacles, they give up. They believe the words of the negative people who tell them that they cannot successfully pursue their dream. Throughout history, the world has been filled with potentially great people who gave up too soon. That means many people die without having reached their potential.

Fortunately, though, the world has seen many others who did persevere—like Polish pianist Ignace Paderewski. When he first chose to play the piano, he was told by his music teacher that his hands were too small to master the keyboard. Or Enrico Caruso, the great Italian tenor, who was told when he first applied for musical instruction that his voice was like the wind whistling through a window. Another person who persevered was the great statesman of Victorian England, Benjamin Disraeli. The first time he attempted to speak in Parliament, members hissed him into silence. They laughed when he said, "Though I sit down now, the time will come when you will hear of me." But because he didn't give up, they did hear from him later—as a member of Parliament, and two-time Prime Minister.

FORMULA FOR OVERCOMING FAILURE

Time after time, great achievers are people who tenaciously overcome their failures to pursue their dreams. They are persistent, and they formulate strategies for success. If you desire to be successful, you too must develop a strategy for overcoming failure. Here are some tips I believe will help you:

RECOGNIZE FAILURE FOR WHAT IT IS

The first step in overcoming failure is recognizing it for what it is: a temporary setback. Failure is not final—unless you make it final. Delays need not be deadly. Pressures are not permanent. Failures should be viewed as mileage markers on the road to success, not nails in a coffin. How you see failure is entirely a function of your attitude.

Great achievers are people who tenaciously overcome their failures to pursue their dreams.

REVIEW YOUR FAILURE IN ORDER TO LEARN

"Failure should be our teacher, not our undertaker," said William A. Ward. "Failure is delay, not defeat.... It is a temporary detour, not a dead-end street." When you are able to view failure as an opportunity or delay, you're freed to take the second important step in overcoming it: learning from it.

Unsuccessful people try once, don't succeed, and then give up, turning their attention to something else. They live by this amusing motto: "If at first you don't succeed, destroy all evidence that you tried and failed." On the other hand, if successful people try once and don't succeed, they review their failure in order to learn. Then they try the same task again. If necessary, they even repeat the process to continue learning from their mistakes. And because of their perseverance, they eventually succeed.

The next time you fail, review what happened and try objectively to discern what caused the failure. By examining your mistakes and making adjustments, you will be better able to try again. And this time, you will be wiser and better equipped to succeed.

28

RECOGNIZE YOUR WEAKNESSES

This is the most difficult part of learning from your failures. Finding and facing your own personal weaknesses takes genuine honesty and real character. But it is often necessary to lasting success. That's because once you recognize a personal weakness, and begin using self-discipline to correct it, you grow as a person. As a result, you're less likely to be hindered by that weakness in the future.

I've discovered examples of this process in the lives of many people from history. One of the best is the life of Lord Nelson, an admiral who became one of England's most famous naval heroes. He suffered from seasickness throughout his entire life. Needless to say, the man whose fleet destroyed Napoleon's did not let his weakness interfere with his career. He not only learned to live with it, but he conquered it.

Most of us have our own version of "seasickness." For some the problem may be physical—for others psychological. Usually the discipline of overcoming it is a private war carried on quietly within ourselves. It is something we will never receive a medal for. But when we do succeed, nothing can dim the satisfaction of knowing that we persevered and didn't let a personal failure cause defeat.

READJUST YOUR EFFORTS

This is another important part of the process of overcoming failure, because you cannot overcome failure by repeating the same flawed process over and over. Yet so many people do just that. *They repeat the same mistakes, and yet expect different results.*

I am reminded of a story told by an eminent plastic surgeon who met with a young patient who had lost his hand at the wrist. But when the doctor asked the young man about his handicap, the boy replied, "I don't have a handicap, sir. I just don't have a right hand."

The surgeon later found out that this boy was one of the leading scorers on his high school American football team. The teenager didn't allow an obvious shortcoming to make him give up. He simply made the adjustments necessary in order to succeed.

REENTER THE GAME

This brings me to the last point in the strategy for overcoming failure. When all the analysis is done and the adjustments are made, just like the boy without the hand, you still need to get back into the game. If you don't, you will never have the opportunity to succeed.

Fletcher L. Byrom said, "It's a cliché to say that we learn by our mistakes, but I'll state the case more strongly than that: I'll say you can't learn without mistakes." It may sound strange, but you can often measure your willingness to learn by the number of mistakes you make. If you look back at the end of a year and can say to yourself, "I didn't make any mistakes," then you probably haven't stretched yourself enough. If you can say, "I made many mistakes, but I did it while trying to stretch, grow and risk," then you are probably learning and progressing in your growth.

When you live on the cutting edge, you make a great deal of progress. But you also make many mistakes. If you're learning from those mistakes, then you are probably on the road to greater success.

THE SEEDS OF DISCOURAGEMENT

One of the great challenges of people who continually strive for success is the discouragement that can come with failure. But while everyone experiences failure—since it cannot be avoided—not everyone needs to experience discouragement. Failure is external. It involves not achieving a goal or succeeding in a task. Discouragement, on the other hand, is internal. It's a mental attitude, and mental attitudes can be controlled.

All of us have the seeds of discouragement sown in our lives. But we can choose what we will do with them. Will we water and feed those seeds of discouragement, allowing them to grow and eventually choke us to death, or will we starve them so that they don't have a chance to grow and hurt us?

Here are four of the most common seeds of discouragement. By recognizing them for what they are, you can take action to prevent them from growing into full-blown discouragement:

1. FOCUS ON SELF

Selfishness is one of the most prevalent causes of discouragement. When a person is focused on himself and measures life's daily events only in terms of their benefits to him, he waters the seeds of discouragement.

It's not uncommon for counselors to advise people who are discouraged or depressed to spend time among other people (especially among those less fortunate than themselves) and do things for them. This is often good advice, because it takes the discouraged person's focus off of himself. And as his selfishness decreases, so does his level of discouragement.

If you get discouraged easily, try to spend time regularly helping and serving others. As you benefit those around you, you also help yourself.

2. THE BELIEF THAT OPPORTUNITY IS GONE

Few things discourage a person more quickly than the belief that opportunity is gone. Loss of opportunity can lead to loss of hope. And loss of hope tends to lead to discouragement.

Keep in mind that opportunity always looks bigger going than coming. It's much easier to see a missed opportunity than one that hasn't yet come. But new opportunities are always on the horizon, whether we currently see them or not.

*Opportunity always looks
bigger going than coming.*

It's easy to get discouraged when you can only see past opportunities. To overcome discouragement, take action in these areas:

• *Maintain Your Perspective.* If you can keep in mind that new opportunities are always on their way, you'll spend less time worrying about the ones you missed. Discouragement cannot flourish in an attitude of expectation.

• *Learn to Recognize Opportunities As They Arrive.* If you train yourself to see opportunities, you will be able to seize them. Learn to have an eye for opportunities by talking to successful people. Ask them how they recognized their ideas. Read books on great men and learn from their experiences. Consistently cultivate an attitude of openness, willing to accept and act on opportunities as they arrive.

31

3. THE BELIEF THAT SUCCESS SHOULD BE IMMEDIATE

Our culture promotes the idea that *everyone* is an overnight success. But in reality, success rarely comes in a moment. It is the result of continuous, steady effort—over time. Once you make that discovery, you are less likely to become discouraged when you do not succeed overnight.

A study conducted by the National Retail Dry Goods Association in the United States made the following observations about salesmen and rejection:

48% of all salesmen make one call and stop.

25% of all salesmen make two calls and stop.

15% of all salesmen make three calls and stop.

12% of all salesmen make three calls and continue making calls.

This means that if that first call is rejected, nearly half of all salesmen never try again. In fact, the persistence is so important in that field that the 12% who keep trying after three rejections are responsible for 80% of all sales that take place.

George H. Mathason said, "We conquer - not in any brilliant fashion - we conquer by continuing!" The value of courage, persistence, and perseverance has rarely been illustrated more convincingly than in the life story of this man:

At age 22, he failed in business.

At age 23, he ran for the state legislature and was defeated.

At age 24, he again failed in business.

At age 25, he was elected to the state legislature.

At age 26, he experienced the death of his sweetheart.

At age 27, he had a nervous breakdown.

At age 29, he was defeated for the position of house speaker.

At age 31, he was defeated for the position of elector.

At age 34, he was defeated for Congress.

At age 37, he was elected to Congress.

At age 39, he was defeated for Congress.

At age 46, he was defeated for the Senate.

At age 47, he was defeated for the Vice Presidency.

At age 49, he was again defeated for the Senate.

At age 51, he was elected President of the United States.

That man was Abraham Lincoln, considered by many people to be the greatest President of the United States. Yet in a span of almost thirty years, he experience at least 12 major failures. He persisted because he knew that success in reaching his goals would take time and dedication.

Most "overnight successes" have spent years working to get where they are.

It's important to remember that there is no guarantee that success will be immediate. It usually takes time. Most "overnight successes" have spent years working to get where they are. They are people who continued to persevere, knowing that success comes to those who don't get discouraged.

4. LACK OF PURPOSE AND A PLAN

Thomas A. Edison, inventor of the light bulb, phonograph, and thousands of other inventions, described five factors that he considered the most important in inventing:

1. The ability to define what is to be achieved.
2. The ability to fix your mind on that purpose, using all the resources at your command in order achieve it.
3. The ability to keep searching for a way to succeed no matter how many setbacks you encounter.
4. The ability to persevere in light of the knowledge that someone else may have tried and failed using a similar idea or method.
5. The ability to believe that the solution exists and that you will find it if you persevere.

Edison was a man who refused to become discouraged. Even when his laboratory and everything in it was destroyed in a fire, he didn't consider quitting. He saw it as an opportunity to rebuild and start again, only better than before.

OVERCOMING DISCOURAGEMENT

Maybe you or someone you know is already feeling discouraged. And maybe you don't know what to do about it. Don't despair. Anyone can change from discouraged to encouraged. Here are four steps that can help:

1. TAKE POSITIVE ACTION

As I mentioned earlier, if you wait until you feel like acting before you do it, you never will. You must act first, and the feelings will follow.

I once heard the story of a poet who, while walking in his garden, saw a birds' nest lying on the ground. A storm had come through the previous night and swept the nest out of a nearby tree. As the poet mused sadly over the wreckage of the nest, he looked into the tree for its owners. He found the birds easily, but to his surprise, they weren't perched above, staring dejectedly at their ruined home. Instead, they were fluttering around in search of building materials for a new one. The poet observed that the birds didn't let the storm's destruction discourage them. Instead, they took positive action.

2. START THINKING POSITIVELY

One of the most famous American racehorses of all time was named Man o'War. The powerful thoroughbred won many races in his career, posting six consecutive wins in his two-year-old season alone. And he won many of his races by a huge margin, often leading from start to finish. But in 1919, the unthinkable happened. He lost for the first time—and to a horse named Upset. Here's how it happened.

Before the race began, the horses were left waiting at the gate for about five minutes—an unusually long time. Because of the wait, Man o'War, who was always skittish before any race, wasn't paying attention when the starter's pistol fired, and he started very poorly. Upon leaving the starting gate, he was running all the way back in fifth place—in a seven-horse race.

Thoroughbred horses can be temperamental, and some that are used to winning give up after a poor start. But not Man o'War. He gallantly tried to make up the distance. By the time the race reached the halfway mark, he had moved from fifth to fourth position. He was in third place by the three-quarter pole. And when the horses turned into the final stretch, he had moved into a strong second. Just ten lengths from the finish line, Man o'War's head was even with Upset's saddle, and he was still advancing when they crossed the finish line. Upset came in first, staging the "upset" of the century. But had the race been just a little longer, Man o'War would have won. And that's not the end of the story. One year later, Man 'O War raced Upset again, this time beating him soundly.

Man o' War was a great horse because he wanted to win, even when the odds were against him. He never gave up. If you desire to overcome discouragement, believe that you can win the race. Don't ever believe you've lost, or you already have.

3. STUDY POSITIVE EXAMPLES

One of the best ways to fight discouragement is to study examples of positive, persistent people and then emulate them. The people you study can be achievers you know personally. Or you can read biographies and examine the people's lives for qualities you admire and learn how they cultivated those qualities. You can find examples almost anywhere.

> *One of the best ways to fight discouragement is to study examples of positive, persistent people, and then emulate them..*

I enjoy the story of the fourteenth-century Mongol emperor Tamerlane who was once inspired by a positive example he observed in nature. His army had been routed—dispersed by a powerful enemy. The emperor himself lay hidden in a deserted manger while enemy troops scoured the countryside.

As he lay there, desperate and dejected, Tamerlane watched an ant try to carry a grain of corn over a perpendicular wall. The kernel was larger than the ant itself. Sixty-nine times the ant tried to carry it up the wall. Sixty-nine times he fell back. On the seventieth try, he pushed the grain of corn over the top.

Tamerlane leaped to his feet with a shout! He, too, would triumph in the end! And he did—he reorganized his forces and put the enemy to flight. In the end, his empire extended over much of Asia, covering thousands of miles.

4. DEVELOP POSITIVE PERSISTENCE

Persistent effort seems to be one of the most important ingredients for personal success. Napoleon Hill, author of *Think and Grow Rich*, studied the lives of more than 500 of the most successful men in America and got to know many of them personally. He found one indispensable ingredient that was common in all of their success stories: persistence. These individuals kept trying even after repeated failures. It seemed to him that great success was won only by people who overcame incredible obstacles and great discouragement. His observation is similar to one made by American inventor Booker T. Washington: "I have learned that success is to be measured not so much by the position that one has reached in life as by the obstacles which one has overcome while trying to succeed."

Harold Sherman once wrote a book entitled *How To Turn Failure Into Success*. In it he gave the following "Code of Persistence":

1. I will never give up so long as I know I am right.
2. I will believe that all things will work out for me if I hang on to the end.
3. I will be courageous and undismayed in the face of poor odds.
4. I will not permit anyone to intimidate or deter me from my goals.
5. I will fight to overcome all physical handicaps and setbacks.
6. I will try again and again and yet again to accomplish what I desire.
7. I will take new faith and resolution from the knowledge that all successful men and women have had to fight defeat and adversity.
8. I will never surrender to discouragement or despair no matter what seeming obstacles may confront me.

---

*Never underestimate
the importance of
persistence.*

36

When trying to become successful, never underestimate the importance of persistence. It is one of the best weapons against discouragement. Here are seven qualities that help a person develop persistence:

A DEFINITE PURPOSE. Knowing what you want is the first and perhaps most important step toward achieving goals. Strong motives help you surmount difficulties.

DESIRE. It is easier to develop and maintain persistence when pursuing something you intensely desire.

SPECIFIC GOALS. Organized goals and plans always encourage you to "stick it out."

ACCURATE KNOWLEDGE. Nothing can take the place of doing your homework. Knowing that your plans are sound (based upon experience or observation) encourages assurance and persistence. Just guessing has the opposite effect.

COOPERATION. Maintaining an attitude of sympathy, understanding and harmonious cooperation creates connections, giving a support system to help you continue..

WILLPOWER. Concentrating on completing plans for a definite purpose takes your eyes off obstacles and leads to persistence.

HABIT. The mind absorbs and becomes a part of what it experiences daily.

People who maintain a positive attitude can enjoy life no matter where they are or what they're doing. But also being able to overcome failure and avoid discouragement provides the additional advantage of being able to grow and move forward. By conquering failure and discouragement, you can pursue your dreams and achieve success, just like this man:

In 1490, Queen Isabella and King Ferdinand of Spain commissioned a royal committee, with the purpose of examining Christopher Columbus' plan to find a new and shorter route to the fabled Indies.

The committee, an impressive panel of experts headed by Spain's leading geographers and scholars, studied Columbus' scheme and presented their findings to the King and Queen.

Columbus' plan, they said, could not be accomplished. They decided that it was impossible.

Fortunately, Isabella, Ferdinand and, more importantly, Columbus himself, were able to remain encouraged despite this potential failure. They ignored the experts, and the Nina, the Pinta, and the Santa Maria set sail. You know the rest of the story. Columbus proved that the world was not flat, but a globe. He discovered unknown continents, and the course of human history changed radically.

History abounds with tales of experts who were convinced that the obtainable was impossible. It is fortunate that men and women like Columbus disregarded the experts, overcame failure, and achieved success anyway. They did it, and so can you.

SUCCESS STRATEGY ACTIVITIES

1. Identify your last failure and determine to learn from it by asking yourself the following questions:

 a. What exactly caused me to fail?
 b. What can I do next time in a similar situation that will improve my chances of success?
 c Did an area of personal weakness contribute to my failure? If the answer is "yes," what is my plan to overcome that weakness?
 d. What must I do to "get back into the game" if I haven't already done so?

2. Failures can often lead to unexpected opportunities. Examine your life for past failures that ultimately gave you opportunities that you would have otherwise missed. Based on those observations, think about what opportunities may surface as a result of recent or current failures. What can you do to seize those upcoming opportunities?

3. Pick three successful people that you know. Make appointments to interview them and find out how they recognized the opportunities they seized. You may even want to ask them whether they see any opportunities currently on the horizon that would be suitable for you to take advantage of.

4. Read biographies of people you admire for their tenacity and ability to overcome failure. Write down the personal characteristics and habits they cultivated in order to be successful. Then determine how you can cultivate those same characteristics in your life.

5. Write your own personal code of persistence (similar to the one written by Harold Sherman). Post your code where you can see it every day. Evaluate yourself periodically to determine whether or not you are living up to it.

———————

-chapter three-

The Successful Person Possesses . . .

VISION

Poor eyes limit your sight; poor vision limits your deeds.

—Franklin Field

A blind man's world is bounded by the limits of his touch; an ignorant man's world by the limits of his knowledge; a great man's world by the limits of his vision.

—E. Paul Hovey

THE VALUE OF A VISION

The people who have most powerfully and permanently influenced their generation have been "seers"—men and women who see more and farther than others. The people who make things happen are those who have vision.

Webster's *New World Dictionary of the English Language* defines *vision* as "something supposedly seen by other than normal sight; . . . the ability to perceive something not actually visible, as through mental acuteness, keen foresight . . . force or power of imagination."

> *The people who make things happen*
> *are those who have vision.*

In the literal sense, vision is the ability to see physical objects. But less literally, it is also seeing beyond the physical. Sometimes we call it the ability to "read between the lines"- to see significance that may not be readily apparent to others. In other words, a person with vision can see opportunity.

Vision can refer to the ability to visualize the future—not in a mystical or prophetic way, but in an imaginative way. Author

40

George Barna said, "Vision is a picture in your mind's eye of the way things could or should be in the days ahead."

Walt Disney exemplified that kind of vision. He could conceptualize a place where imagination was key, where children would be delighted, and where families could spend time together exploring new worlds. It was a place where fictional places and people tangibly came to life. And Disney's vision eventually became a reality, first at Disneyland in California, then at Disneyworld in Florida, and finally in two more parks in Japan and France.

A person without vision sees only what is immediate, what he can contain, and what is convenient. Someone with vision, on the other hand, has the whole world open to him. Katherine Logan said, "A vision foretells what may be ours. It is an invitation to do something. With a great mental picture in mind we go from one accomplishment to another, using the materials about us only as steppingstones to that which is higher and better and more satisfying. We thus become possessors of the unseen values which are eternal."

*The greater the vision, the
greater the potential
it gives.*

Vision brings great benefits and opens incredible doors of opportunity. It increases a person's potential. The greater the vision, the greater the potential it gives. And it can't be limited by circumstances. A person's occupation doesn't determine his vision; he could be a truck driver, banker, college president, clerk, or farmer.

The importance of vision to success has long been known. The statement, "Where there is no vision, the people perish," was written and recorded in Proverbs 29:18 of the Bible approximately 3,000 years ago. Despite the continuing value of vision, it seems to be a scarce quality in people today.

OBSTRUCTIONS TO VISION

Developing vision, much like a good attitude, is not genetic. Very few of us are born with the ability to see opportunities and visualize a positive future. Instead, vision needs to be cultivated. And like a delicate plant, it can be squashed. Here are five common factors that can limit our vision:

1. OUR PAST

Our past has incredible potential to limit us, since we tend to view future possibilities through the filter of past successes or failures. If you have had a particularly difficult, traumatic, or unsuccessful past, you will probably have to work harder to broaden your vision for the future.

A great example from nature of this truth can be seen in the workings of a flea circus. You may have seen one before at a carnival or circus. The tiny insects make tremendous leaps as they perform, yet never go beyond a predetermined height. Each flea seems to recognize an invisible ceiling. Why do they limit their jumps? Because when they're being trained, fleas are placed under a glass dome. For a while, they try to jump out, smashing against the glass ceiling. After numerous failed attempts, they finally stop trying to escape. At that point, a large portion of their training is complete. Later, even when the glass is removed, they don't try to jump beyond the height of the dome. Their past experience has led them to believe that they can't get out. Thus, they become victims of their own imagined limitations.

Be prepared to dream big and then test your limits. Don't put a lid on your potential.

People can respond in the same way to past limitations. If you believe strongly enough that you can't succeed, then you will put limits on your vision. But even if there was a lid in the past, it's probably been removed. Be prepared to dream big and then test your limits. Don't put a lid on your potential.

2. CURRENT PRESSURES

I once read about a father and son who took their donkey to the market one day in order to buy food. At first, the father sat on the donkey and the boy walked. But as they traveled, onlookers remarked: "What a terrible thing, a big strong man like that riding while the poor boy has to walk."

So at the next opportunity, the father got off and let the boy ride. But then people said: "How disrespectful. The father walks while his son rides."

So then they both got on the donkey's back. The people's comment? "How cruel! Two people riding on that poor donkey's back."

Hearing this, they both got off the donkey and walked. But then passers-by snickered, "How foolish they are. Both of them walk while a perfectly healthy donkey has nothing on his back."

The father and son finally arrived at the market—a day late. And when they entered, everyone stopped and stared. They'd never before seen a man and boy arrive at the market carrying a donkey!

Like the man with the donkey, we can become so concerned with outside pressures that we lose sight of where we're going and why we're going there. Trivial affairs and hollow criticism can preoccupy us so completely that there is no room in our minds for vision.

3. PROBLEMS

Dare to dream—in spite of problems, circumstances, and handicaps. History is filled with great men and women who faced their problems and achieved success in spite of them.

Dare to dream—
in spite of problems, circumstances,
and handicaps.

For example, Demosthenes, the greatest orator of the ancient world, stuttered! The first time he tried to make a public speech, he was laughed off the rostrum. But he had a vision of being a great speaker. It is said that he would put pebbles in his mouth and practice speaking over the noise of the crashing surf at the seashore.

Other men overcame problems to fulfill their visions: Julius Caesar, despite being an epileptic, became a general and later an emperor. Napoleon, despite his humble parentage, also became an emperor. Beethoven brought to life his inner vision for music when

43

he composed symphonies while deaf. Charles Dickens had a vision to become a writer and became the greatest novelist of Victorian England despite being lame and born into poverty.

Everyone has problems. Some are shortcomings we were born with. Others are problems we've created for ourselves. No matter what yours are, don't allow them to destroy your vision for the future.

4. LACK OF PERSPECTIVE

Perspective is invaluable to good vision. After all, what is vision but a view of present circumstances and future prospects in relation to a bigger picture of life?

I once heard the story of the late Lord Northcliffe of England, editor and owner of the *London Times*. At one point in his life, he was threatened with complete blindness. But when his eyes were examined by specialists, nothing could be found wrong with them. After learning what type of work he had been doing, the specialists concluded that he needed to change his perspective by looking at far-away objects. He had been using his eyes too much for reading fine print and for close observation.

Lord Northcliffe was advised to spend time in the country, away from the printed page, where he could look on vast horizons of God's creation. This simple remedy corrected his eye trouble.

Lack of perspective is incredibly limiting. Did you know that in the 1800s, someone in the United States Patent Office suggested that the office be closed because he felt nothing else of value could be invented? When we think about the technological advances that have been made since 1900, it seems unbelievable that anyone could have made such a recommendation.

If you have problems with perspective, try to see things from a different point of view. Study history. Study other cultures. Then look at the present with an eye toward the future. As Frank Gaines said, "Only he who can see the invisible can do the impossible."

5. OUR PRESENT POSITION

Oliver Wendell Holmes said, "The great thing in this world is not so much where we are but in what direction we are moving." None of us chooses where, when, or how we begin life. We are born into a situation totally outside of our control. But as we get older, we have more choices. We can pick where we live, whom we marry, what work we do. We choose our direction in life. The older we get, the more choices we have made in our lives, and the more responsibility we have for the outcome.

Many people don't seem to understand this. They believe that their current position in life dictates their destiny. Thus, they have resigned themselves to their condition and believe that they have no choices.

Dream big.
Success is never achieved by men and
women of caution.

Don't fall into that trap. Hundreds of years ago that might have been true, but it isn't now. Nearly anything is possible if you desire it enough and are willing to pay the price to get it. Don't allow your present position, no matter how limited it may seem, to rob you of vision. Success is never achieved by men and women of caution. So dream big.

REALIZING YOUR VISION

Believing that you can improve yourself and your life is only a first step. To be truly valuable, your vision must be accompanied by another quality: the ability to see how to make that future come true. A visionary who cannot make his vision a reality is only a dreamer.

What is needed is a strategy for realizing your vision. Here are some guidelines that will help you:

DEFINE YOUR VISION

This concept is so simple that I'm almost embarrassed to mention it, but realizing a vision always begins with defining it. For some people this is incredibly easy, because they seem to have been born with a vision for their lives. For others, it takes a great deal of time, contemplation, reflection, and prayer.

Your vision must be based on your talents, dreams, hopes, and passions. And if you wish to become successful, you must claim it

45

as yours alone. That's because only when the vision is your own will you have the drive and determination to pursue it. Visions are extraordinary and impact others positively—especially when a person's vision matches his destiny—the purpose for which he was born.

EXAMINE YOUR LIFE AT THE MOMENT

Making your vision become a reality won't be instantaneous. It will be a process, much like taking a journey. And when you decide to take a journey, one of the first tasks is identifying your starting point. Without knowing that, you'll never be able to plot a course to your destination. So take time to assess realistically your personality, skills, gifts, desires, and experiences that make you who you are today. By being honest about your starting point, you'll be able to travel in the right direction.

---

*A visionary who cannot make his vision
a reality is only a dreamer.*

After determining where you are, ask yourself, "How far am I from where I want to be?" In general, the farther away you are from your vision, the longer it will take you to fulfill it—and the greater the cost to you personally. Achieving a vision involves sacrifice, so use the information you get to plan out your route and count the cost of your journey.

EXCHANGE ALL THE LITTLE OPTIONS FOR THE ONE BIG VISION

All dreams have a price. In order to fulfill your vision, you may have to sacrifice some options. You cannot pursue your dream and keep all of your options open at the same time.

---

*You cannot pursue your dream and keep all of
your options open at the same time.*

This concept is especially difficult for Americans to accept. The culture in the United States places a very high value on options; in fact, the entire free market system is based on it. But while options

46

can be good because they present opportunities, at some point, if we want to achieve success, we have to surrender some possibilities. By eliminating some choices, we're free to pursue a single vision.

Yogi Berra once said, "When you come to a fork in the road, take it." Now that sounds pretty obvious. But when faced with a fork in the road in our journey toward our vision, some of us sit down in the middle of the highway and refuse to choose a direction. And by "keeping our options open," we stay where we are—and make no progress.

TAILOR YOUR PERSONAL GROWTH TO YOUR VISION

Part of realizing your vision involves the journey of personal growth that you must take in order to get there. Anyone who believes that he can progress from his current place in life to another place without having to make changes is fooling himself. Positive changes in life always require personal growth.

Since personal growth will be necessary in order to realize your vision, the most strategic plan to have is one that tailors your growth to your vision. Think about what kind of person you will need to become to realize your vision. How far are you from that goal? Make a list of all the changes that need to take place for you to become that person. Then, from your list, create a personal growth plan that includes goals, descriptions and resources. Finally, commit to working on that growth plan every day.

Positive changes in a person's life always require personal growth.

SPEND TIME WITH SUCCESSFUL PEOPLE

One of the best ways to learn to be successful is to spend time with successful people. So involve others in your growth process. Get together with people who are achieving success, and learn from them. Observe them. Ask them questions. Make an effort to learn to think more like them. Remember, the old adage is true: Birds of a feather really do flock together.

CONTINUALLY EXPRESS YOUR BELIEF IN YOUR VISION

Realizing your vision will require both perseverance and momentum. These two traits will keep you motivated throughout the growth process. And continually expressing your belief in your vision is a great way to promote them.

Express your belief to others as well as to yourself. This positive and confident attitude will remind you of your dreams and convince you that it's possible.

EXPECT OPPOSITION TO YOUR VISION

One important reason to remain positive about your vision is the opposition that you'll face. People who have no dream of their own won't be able to see yours. So to them, your vision will be an impossibility. They will tell you that it has no value, or if they can see its value, they may tell you that it might be accomplished, *but not by you.*

People who have no dream of their own won't be able to see yours.

If you're not surprised when opposition comes, you'll be able to deflect it. Have an unsinkable positive attitude.

EXCLUDE NEGATIVE THINKERS AS CLOSE FRIENDS

You will have to face people who will criticize you and doubt your vision, but that doesn't mean that you have to take these people into your confidence or embrace them as close friends. Treat everyone you meet with kindness and compassion, even if they're negative, but don't pursue negative people as close friends. If you do, as they continue to share their doubt and negative outlook with you, you will begin believing them. And once you *believe* that your dream is out of your reach, it will *be* out of your reach.

EXPLORE EVERY POSSIBLE AVENUE TO FULFILL YOUR VISION

In order to realize your vision, you must continually look for anything that can help you. Be willing to try new things. Look everywhere for ideas. Be observant. Ideas that work successfully in another area may be useful in your plan. Keep your focus fixed on your vision, but remain flexible about the road you will take to get there. The realization of a vision requires innovation, and that means being open to new ideas.

Keep your focus fixed on your vision, but remain flexible about the road you will take to get there.

EXCEED NORMAL EXPECTATIONS

All of the strategies I've already mentioned can help you to realize your vision, but they won't do you much good if you're not willing to go above and beyond what is normally expected of you. No one achieves his dreams with average energy and effort. It takes dedication and continued effort. When you're willing to pay that price, you'll also succeed beyond normal expectations.

HELP OTHERS WHO HAVE A SIMILAR VISION

This final strategy may seem like a "nice idea," but not really necessary. But it's essential. In order to realize your vision and fulfill you dreams, you must help other people. But why? Contrary to popular belief, helping others does not waste valuable time and energy that could be used to achieve success. Time spent in helping others is never wasted, because without other people there can be no success. If you want to extend your success beyond your own circle and lifetime, that can only be accomplished through others.

Without other people there can be no success.

Helping others improves the quality of life, for you and for those around you. And when you help others who have a similar vision to yours, it also creates a special win-win situation. As you help them get what they want, they generally desire to help you in return. Plus, both of you learn from one another.

Even when others don't help you in return, you will have made a positive contribution to another life—extending your influence and success.

Vision provides the creative spark that makes great achievements possible. As John Jay Chapman said, "The world values the seer [the person with vision] above all men, and has always done so. . . . With Beethoven's symphonies, with Adam Smith's *Wealth of Nations*—with any conceivable output of the human mind of which you approve . . . you love them because you say . . . 'These things were not made, they were seen.'" The ideas first existed in the minds and hearts of the great men who envisioned them.

> *Vision provides the creative spark that makes great achievements possible.*

That's the way it is with anyone who achieves success. The Olympic athlete who achieves the gold medal does so not simply because of athletic skill, but through the power of the vision that drives him. The same is true of the business leader. Vision is the dream that will propel you forward. And the achievement of that dream will define for you many of the elements of success.

Without vision, there is nothing to shoot for, no target, no greater task to give you purpose and hope. As Douglas Lurtan said, "When you determine what you want, you have made the most important decision in your life. You have to know what you want in order to attain it." When you develop vision, you're able to see what you want to accomplish. With vision, you will have a driving force that gives you a reason to keep going during the bad times as well as the good. It will enable you to accomplish that which is greater than you are.

Dream big. Only when your dreams are great can your accomplishment be great.

SUCCESS STRATEGY ACTIVITIES

1. Set aside a day to think, reflect, and pray about a vision for your life. Plan to get away from all distractions and interruptions. You may want to travel out to the country, rent a hotel room, or go some other place where you can enjoy solitude.

Take with you paper and pen, your calendar, and any books that may help you (such as a Bible if you are a Christian). Once you are alone, ask yourself the following questions, and write down your answers:

    a. What are my talents and gifts? What is it that I can do better than anything else or better than anyone else I know?

    b. What is my passion? Is there something that touches my heart and gives me added energy to work and accomplish? If so, what is it?

    c. What is unique about my personal history? What life experiences do I have that make me unique and give me special insights, experience, and abilities? What can I do that is out of the ordinary?

    d. What is unique about the time and place I live in? Vision often emerges as a part the unique circumstances of a person's life. Geography, political climate, history, economics, cultural background, and a multitude of other factors can all play a part. Write down anything that could influence your opportunities.

    e. What significant people am I in contact with? The talents, gifts, and passions of others with whom you could collaborate may present opportunities you might not be able to realize alone.

    f. What needs do I see that I would like to see filled? Often the desire to meet a need can fuel a vision.

    g. What is the greatest thing I can imagine myself doing in my life time?

Repeat this process once a year or as often as you need to do it. You will probably find that your vision changes over the years. If you go several years with the same vision, and that vision is large—larger than you think you can accomplish—it is likely that you've focused in on a good vision for your life. You may discover in the years to come that it only becomes modified or expanded; it doesn't change dramatically.

2.   Set aside several hours to review your current business situation with the goal of discovering a new vision for it that you had not previously considered. Follow the same guidelines as in activity number one: Find a place of solitude and take with you the materials you will need. Then write down your answers to the following questions:
   a. What talents, gifts, and resources do I possess that I am not currently utilizing?
   b. How does the uniqueness of the time and place I live in affect my current business situation?
   c. What opportunities do I have that are a result of my answer to the previous question?
   d. If I had unlimited resources and knew that all my efforts could succeed, what would be my business goal? *Remember—dream big!*
   e. Who do I know with a similar vision? How can I help them, and how can they help me?

-chapter four-

The Successful Person Sets ...
GOALS

To achieve happiness, we should make certain that we are never without an important goal.

—*Earl Nightingale*

The world makes way for the man who knows where he is going.

—*Ralph Waldo Emerson*

By now you're probably beginning to see a pattern in the strategies for success offered in this book. The whole concept of achieving success begins with you—with how positively you think. Added to that is a determination to overcome failure. Those attitudes provide the ability to see nearly limitless possibilities and opportunities in everything around you. In time, you are able to develop not only the vision which empowers you in your day to day activities, but also to develop a more specific, all-encompassing vision for your life.

*To achieve success
you need to develop goals.*

Right thinking creates a solid foundation for success. But it is only the first step. Once you have formed that foundation, you are ready to begin building on it. In order to achieve success, you will need to develop goals.

GOALS: THE BUILDING BLOCKS OF SUCCESS

Up to now, we've talked quite a bit about success, but we haven't identified what it means to be successful. Ask ten people to define success, and you will probably get ten different answers. To one person it involves earning a certain amount of money. To another, success means being an excellent parent. Yet another person will say that he is successful if he reaches his potential in his profession. Take a look at this satirical description of the successful person:

The practical person is the one who knows how to get what he wants;

The philosopher is the one who knows what people ought to want; and

The successful person is the one who knows how to get what he ought to want.

---

*Success is the progressive
realization of a worthwhile,
predetermined goal.*

One of the best definitions of success that I've ever heard is this: Success is the progressive realization of a worthwhile, predetermined goal. This definition can work for anyone, no matter what his focus is in life. It allows you to tailor success to your personal values and vision. At the same time, you can see how incredibly important goals are. Without defined goals, success is unattainable, because success is actually the attainment of those goals.

Goals do even more than just identify the desired end result. They help all along the way. Goals are measurable milestones along the road to success. Their value is tremendous.

GOALS MOTIVATE US

When you set goals for yourself, they work in two ways: you work on them and they work on you. Goals give you a tangible target to shoot for. And as you make progress on them, you gain a sense of accomplishment. For that reason, good goals are always measurable. When you have an unmeasurable goal—so that you can't judge your progress—it actually reduces motivation. If you can't measure your progress, you will become demoralized and give up.

Let me give you a real-life example on the motivating power of a measurable goal.

The California Coast was shrouded in fog on the morning of July 4, 1952. Twenty-one miles to the west on Catalina Island, a 34-year-old woman waded into the Pacific Ocean and began swimming toward the coastline. If she succeeded, she would be the first woman to do so. Her name was Florence Chadwick, and she had already been the first woman to swim the English Channel in both directions.

The water was numbingly cold that morning, and the fog was so thick that Florence could hardly see the boats that accompanied her. As the hours passed, millions across the country breathlessly awaited the outcome. Several times sharks ventured close to her and were driven away with rifles. Still she swam on. Fatigue had never been her greatest problem in these swims; it had always been the bone-chilling cold of the water.

More than fifteen hours after she started, tired and numb with the cold, Florence determined that she could not go on and asked to be taken out of the water. Both her mother and her trainer in a nearby boat told her they were near land and urged her not to quit. But when she looked toward the California Coast, all she could see was fog.

A few minutes later—at fifteen hours and fifty-five minutes—she was taken out of the water. But in a few hours, as her body warmed up, she began to feel the shock of failure. Florence Chadwick exclaimed to a reporter, "Look I'm not excusing myself. But if I could have seen land, I might have made it."

She had been pulled out only half a mile from the California Coast. Later she explained that it was neither fatigue nor cold that had caused her to give up—it was her inability to see her goal because of the fog.

Fortunately, that was the only time Florence Chadwick ever quit. Two months later she swam that same channel successfully. And not only was she the first woman to swim the Catalina Channel, but she also beat the men's record by some two hours!

Florence Chadwick was a great swimmer, but she still needed a goal that she could see to accomplish what she was capable of. Never underestimate the importance of creating measurable goals when planning for your own success.

GOALS GIVE US PURPOSE

Every day we meet people who are unhappy with their lives and the world around them. Did you know that 98 out of 100 people who are dissatisfied with their world do not have a clear picture in their minds of what world they would like?! They have no goal of a better life. They have no purpose that drives them. As a result, they continue to live in a world they make no effort to change.

I once heard a medical doctor speak on the subject of retirement. He had done extensive research on the common characteristics of those persons who lived to be over 100 years old. He asked the audience to think about what factors the long-lived people might have in common. Most audience members expected him to identify such things as diet, exercise, moderation in drinking and smoking, and other activities that might affect the body. However, the doctor surprised the audience by telling them that there were few, if any, commonalities in terms of diet or exercise habits. *The most common factor that he found among those over 100 years of age was their view toward the future: they all had goals.*

Setting goals may not enable you to live to be 100, but it will greatly increase the probability of your being successful. Without a sense of purpose, you are likely to go nowhere in life. As merchandising entrepreneur J.C. Penney said, "Give me a stock clerk with a goal and I will give you a man who will make history. Give me a man without a goal, and I will give you a stock clerk."

*The way people undertake their affairs
is largely determined by the way they see their goals.*

GOALS ADD VALUE TO WORK

The way people undertake their affairs is largely determined by the way they see their goals. When they have goals that they believe are unimportant, then the work they do to accomplish them has little value. But when the goals seem worthwhile, they're excited working to reach them. That's why it's so important to base your goals on *your vision*. When your goals contribute to a vision you value, then the work that accomplishes those goals is also valuable to you.

GOALS KEEP OUR PRIORITIES STRAIGHT

One of the greatest assets of goal setting is that it helps us to keep our priorities straight on a day-to-day basis. Without them, it becomes easy for us to get caught up in activities that do not contribute to our vision. The person who forgets what is ultimately important will become the slave of the immediate. Or as someone once said, "Wisdom is the art of knowing what to overlook."

GOALS CHANNEL AND MAXIMIZE OUR POTENTIAL

Many years ago, a newspaper headline told of 300 whales that suddenly died. The whales had been pursuing sardines and found themselves marooned in a bay. Frederick Brown Harris commented at the time, "The small fish lured the sea giants to their death. They came to their violent demise by chasing small ends, by prostituting vast powers for insignificant goals."

---

*To reach your potential,
you need to emphasize areas of
strength and high return.*

People without goals are similar to those whales. Although they have tremendous power and potential, they expend their energies on small things, which lead them away from what they really should be doing. When it comes right down to it, to reach your potential, you need to emphasize areas of strength and high return.

Goals help you to remain focused. Plus, as you continue to work in areas of strength, you further develop those strengths. In the end, when you reach your goals, what you *get* is not nearly as important as what you *become.*

GOALS GIVE US POWER TO LIVE IN THE PRESENT

Successful people live and work in the present. That is where they have the power to accomplish their goals. As Hilaire Belloc said, "While you are dreaming of the future or regretting the past, the present, which is all you have, slips from you and is gone."

Even though goals look forward—toward accomplishments to be made in the future—they enable us to live in the present. How?

By allowing us to see larger tasks as a series of smaller tasks or steps. Working toward the accomplishment of any vision involves setting and achieving a series of goals. And achieving each goal is the result of achieving smaller goals or steps. So when you focus on the smaller tasks at hand, in the knowledge that they're contributing to your goals in fulfillment of your vision, you can consider yourself successful.

Successful people
live and work in the present.
That is where they have the power
to accomplish their goals.

GOALS HELP US COMMUNICATE

Think about all of the great communicators that you've ever met or heard. One of the things they have in common is an ability to put complex ideas into simple terms. They are able to organize and focus their ideas. As a result, we can understand them better.

Setting goals is a way of putting a complex idea—your vision—into a simpler form—your goals. Thus it organizes the ideas we have for our future. Because those ideas are organized and focused, we can communicate them to others more easily.

GOALS PROMOTE ENTHUSIASM IN AN ORGANIZATION

One of the most common problems I see in struggling organizations is a lack of enthusiasm among workers. Many of them seem to be going through the motions of their jobs with no apparent purpose other that the accomplishment of the mundane task at hand. People without enthusiasm are rarely better than average performers and achievers.

On the other hand, when people in an organization have goals, it lifts their morale and gives them enthusiasm. Goals provide something tangible to be achieved, and a reason for each person's tasks. They give the team something to shoot for. And workers respond positively because they know where the target is.

GOALS HELP US EVALUATE PROGRESS

A common problem among unsuccessful people is that they rarely evaluate their progress. Either they don't realize that self-evaluation is important, or they have no way of measuring how far they've come.

Goals provide a valuable means of evaluation. When your goals are specific and tangible, then you can compare your current progress against your goals. It will keep you from experiencing the predicament of the inventor who worked for a year on his most recent invention. It had hundreds of wheels, cogs, gears, pulleys, belts, and lights, all of which moved or lit up at the touch of a button. But when someone asked, "What does it do?" the inventor replied, "Oh, it doesn't do anything—but doesn't it run beautifully?"

GOALS FORCE US TO PLAN AHEAD

Successful people are more proactive than reactive. In other words, they plan ahead. They don't wait for others to dictate what they do. Other people don't control their calendars.

Planning ahead is the only way to get ahead. For an example, look at Noah from the Bible. He'd never even seen rain. Yet he built the ark before it was absolutely necessary. He didn't wait until it was already raining.

*Planning ahead is the
only way to get ahead.*

Goals serve to help us plan ahead, because they force us to break down what we want to achieve into workable steps. When you want to create a road map to achievement, set goals. As eighteenth century inventor and statesman Benjamin Franklin said in his autobiography, "I have always thought that one man of tolerable abilities may work great changes and accomplish great affairs among mankind, if he first forms a good plan."

GOALS SHIFT OUR EMPHASIS FROM ACTIVITY TO OUTPUT

Unsuccessful people often confuse activity with output. They believe that lots of time spent on activity—especially work that is difficult—brings success. But activity by itself does not guarantee success. It's only beneficial if it's directed toward a positive result. In other words, we must measure our success not by our *activity*, but by our *output*.

One of the best illustrations of this concept that I've ever encountered came from a study done by Jean-Henri Fabre, the great French naturalist. He studied processionary caterpillars, insects that move through the trees in long parades, one after another. In his study, Fabre placed a group of these caterpillars on the rim of a large flowerpot. Each caterpillar was touching the one in front of it, forming a complete circle. Of course, they started moving around in a procession, but since it was a circle, it had neither beginning nor end. Then near the caterpillars, Fabre placed food for them to eat. He knew that to be able to eat, they would have to break ranks and stop following one another. And he expected that after a while they would get tired of their useless march and go for the food. But they didn't.

> *Activity by itself does not guarantee success. It's only beneficial if it's directed toward a positive result.*

Through sheer force of habit, the processionary caterpillars kept moving around the rim of the pot—around and around at the same relentless pace for seven days and seven nights. If allowed to continue, they would have kept going until they starved to death.

Those processionary caterpillars were following instinct, habit, custom, tradition, precedent, past experience, standard practice, or whatever you may choose to call it. But though they were working hard, they got nowhere.

Goals help us keep from mimicking those caterpillars. When you set goals and periodically measure your progress, your focus naturally shifts from activity to output. Simply filling your day with activity no longer seems acceptable. Instead, producing enough output to accomplish your goals becomes the measurement for achievement. And as you reach some of your goals, you learn what it takes to continue succeeding. Often, you realize that you can accomplish more of value in less time. As a result, you discover you can set higher goals and dream bigger dreams. Your effectiveness will increase, and so will your vision for yourself and for others.

When you set goals and periodically measure your progress, your focus naturally shifts from activity to output.

HOW TO START GOAL SETTING

To be effective, goal setting cannot be a one-time activity. No one sets goals, accomplishes them, and then retires. Goals need to be identified, planned, acted upon, and then evaluated on an ongoing basis. Circumstances will require you to be flexible in some areas. As you change, so will your goals. Remember, what happens inside of you as you travel is ultimately more important that just achieving a preset goal.

Everyone has to start somewhere on the road to becoming a goal-oriented person. Most people aren't born that way. Here are six steps you can take to start setting goals:

STEP ONE: IDENTIFY YOUR VISION AND STARTING PLACE

If you have already done the activities at the end of chapter three, you've probably already identified your vision and have a sense of what your starting place is. Knowing both of these is critical to your success. Without a vision, you won't know where you are going. And without knowing your starting place, you can't chart your course. After all, it's possible to have a map and a compass and still be hopelessly lost. A map and a compass are completely useless unless you know the fifth point of the compass—where you are now!

STEP TWO: DEVELOP A CLEAR STATEMENT OF PURPOSE.

You're probably acquainted with the concept of a purpose statement. Effective organizations—businesses, educational institutions, churches, etc.—use them to give their people clear direction. As Bob Townsend said in his book *Up the Organization,* "One of the important functions of a leader is to make the organization concentrate on its objectives." You, too, need something to give you clear direction and help you concentrate on your objectives. If you don't provide it, no one will.

The best way to stay focused is to write a clear statement of purpose for your life. After all, doesn't everyone desire to discover and live his purpose for existence? When you articulate it, you remain focused and effective. Develop your purpose statement based on your vision and your personal convictions. It will help you to make your goals more specific and effective.

The best way to stay focused is to write a clear statement of purpose for your life. After all, doesn't everyone desire to discover and live his purpose for existence?

STEP THREE: TRANSLATE PURPOSE INTO MEASURABLE GOALS

Armed with a vision for the future and your purpose statement, which provide direction, you are ready to begin setting both long- and short-term goals. Goals can be identified by performance (such as the goal of selling 100 units of a product), or by duration (such as the goal of exercising for an hour a day, three days a week for the next year). Depending on what you want to accomplish, your goals can involve any area of your life. Here are examples of areas where you may want to set goals:

Personal Development
Physical Development
Spiritual Development
Professional Accomplishment
Relationships
Family Concerns
Finances

Begin by writing down any goal that comes to you. At first, don't make judgments concerning whether the goals are viable or not. Don't worry about whether they are long-term or short-term. At this point you want to be creative and dream big.

Once you've written down everything you can think of, check your goals against your purpose statement. Ask two questions:

1. Does each goal advance me toward my vision? If you see any goals that are not consistent with your purpose statement and vision for the future, you have two choices–(a) throw it out and forget about it, or (b) reevaluate and consider rewriting your purpose statement. One or the other is necessary, because no one can realize a vision and become successful without goals relevant to that vision.

2. Have I written down the main two-to-five goals necessary in order to realize my vision? This question will help determine whether the goals you have written were inclusive enough. If you see that your vision will require you to pursue additional goals, write those goals down.

Once you have identified some of your goals, you can begin to build a strategy for your success.

Think of your goals as forming a pyramid. Above that pyramid is your statement of purpose. Every goal you set, and all that you do to accomplish those goals, must point to your statement of purpose.

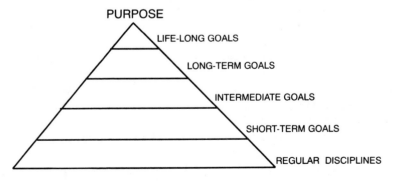

The goal pyramid is made up of five layers. The topmost–the smallest–is the most focused because it contains your life-long goals. The sections beneath contain progressively smaller goals, each contributing to the accomplishment of the goals above them. Here is an overview of each of the five sections:

- Life-long goals: These are the approximately two-to-five things you hope to accomplish in your lifetime. If you are able to achieve them or come close to achieving them, you will have fulfilled to the best of your ability what you believe to be your purpose in life.
- Long-term Goals: These are the goals that you have set to help you reach each of your life-long goals. In general, these are things you hope to accomplish in about ten years. Although it's possible to set goals more than ten years out, it's usually not time spent wisely. That's because the farther away goals are, the less specific and the more subject to change they are.
- Intermediate Goals: These objectives will help you reach each of your long-term goals. In general, these are things you desire to accomplish in five to ten years.
- Short-term Goals: Designed to help you reach each of your intermediate goals, these take from one-to-five years to accomplish.
- Regular Disciplines: These are the tasks to be completed on a daily, weekly, and monthly basis in order to accomplish your short-term goals. These are governed by the way you manage your time (the subject of the next chapter).

STEP FOUR: HEAD INTO ACTION

You can define your purpose and painstakingly set goals for every stage of your life, but if you don't then move into action, you will accomplish nothing.

I once heard about a man who always wanted to visit China. So he decided to plan a trip. First, he spent months reading everything he could about China—its art, history, philosophy, and culture. Then he studied maps of all its provinces. He booked his plane reservations and even planned a detailed itinerary. He finally marked down each place he wanted to visit, accounting for every hour of his journey.

A few days after the man's scheduled return home, a friend who knew how much he was looking forward to his trip stopped by to visit. The friend asked him, "How was China?"

The man replied, "Well, I guess it's fine. I never saw it."

"What?!" cried his friend. "But you spent all that time planning. What happened?"

"Well, I love planning a trip, but I just can't stand going to the airport. So I stayed home."

Contemplating and planning achievements will never satisfactorily replace the attainment of those achievements. Without action, the planner is merely a daydreamer.

You can define your purpose and painstakingly set goals for every stage of your life, but if you don't then move into action, you will accomplish nothing.

STEP FIVE: EVALUATE YOUR PLANS PERIODICALLY

As important as moving into action is periodic evaluation of your progress. Over time, you will sometimes discover that some short-term goals aren't moving you closer to your long-term goals. Or maybe you haven't made your goals realistic enough. You might even decide that one of your long-range goals is not really contributing to your vision and ultimate purpose for your life. No matter what the circumstances are, feel free to make adjustments. The newer this process is to you, the more miscalculations you are likely to make. And the more often you will need to re-evaluate and adjust your goals.

Another problem you might have if you aren't used to working with goals is getting sidetracked. Some people set goals and write out what they must do to accomplish them, and then forget to follow those guidelines. One way to help combat this problem is to post the following sign in your office: "Is what I am doing right now getting me closer to my goal?" Don't forget to read it often and answer honestly.

STEP SIX: CELEBRATE ACCOMPLISHMENTS

Finally, take time to celebrate accomplishments. I've always been a believer in the reward system. When I accomplish some-

65

thing I've set out to do, I give myself a reward. Small accomplishment—small reward. Great accomplishment—big reward. For completing a two-hour task, I might reward myself with a short break, something to eat, or a ball game. What I never do is reward myself before I accomplish what I've set out to do.

When you cultivate the habit of setting and achieving goals, it will mean the difference between accomplishing what is average and achieving more than you thought possible.

THE MILLION-DOLLAR PERSONAL SUCCESS PLAN

Never underestimate the power of goals. When you cultivate the habit of setting and achieving goals, it will mean the difference between accomplishing what is average and achieving more than you thought possible.

Learning to make planning a permanent part of your thinking takes a lot of work. Here is a Million-Dollar Personal Success Plan, designed to help you develop a planning mind-set:

CRYSTALLIZE YOUR THINKING

Determine what specific goal you want to achieve. Then dedicate yourself to its attainment with singleness of purpose.

DEVELOP A PLAN FOR ACHIEVING YOUR GOAL AND A DEADLINE FOR ITS ATTAINMENT

Plan your progress carefully: hour-by-hour, day-by-day, month-by-month. Organized activity and maintained enthusiasm are the wellsprings of your power.

DEVELOP A SINCERE DESIRE FOR THE THINGS YOU WANT IN LIFE

Burning desire is the greatest motivator of every human action. The desire for success instills a "success consciousness," which, in turn, creates a vigorous and ever-increasing habit of success.

DEVELOP SUPREME CONFIDENCE IN YOURSELF AND YOUR OWN ABILITIES

Enter every activity without even acknowledging the possibility of defeat. Concentrate on your strengths, instead of your weaknesses—on your powers, instead of your problems.

DEVELOP A DOGGED DETERMINATION TO FOLLOW THROUGH ON YOUR PLAN

Nothing takes the place of sheer determination. Commit to follow through on your plan regardless of obstacles or criticism, or what other people say, think or do. Strengthen your determination with sustained effort, controlled attention, and concentrated energy.

Opportunities never come to those who wait. They are captured by those who dare to attack. Your ability to attack successfully will be determined by your ability to plan, to set and achieve goals. As pastor and motivational speaker Robert H. Schuller says, "Goals are not only absolutely necessary to motivate us. They are essential to keep us really alive."

Opportunities never come to those who wait. They are captured by those who dare to attack.

Begin setting goals today. Set the course for your future. As Robert F. Mager said, "If you're not sure where you are going, you're liable to end up someplace else." Do everything in your power to fulfill your vision. Don't end up someplace else.

SUCCESS STRATEGY ACTIVITIES

1. Read through the information that you wrote while determining your vision for your life. Based on that vision, write a Statement

of Purpose for yourself. It should be general enough to include all that you wish to do, yet concise. It is something you will memorize. Be sure to include the following:

    a. What the focus of your life's activities will be.

    b. Why you desire to do what you wish to do.

    c. How you intend to accomplish it.

Here are some examples of purpose statements:

> *—I intend to serve others by practicing medicine with the purpose of improving the lives of as many less fortunate people as possible.*

> *—By loving, teaching, and discipling others, I desire to help people find their purpose, develop their commitment, and reach their potential in the body of Christ out of love for and desire to serve God.*

> *—I desire to become financially successful in business by giving my customers the best products and service possible so that I may use my monetary resources to care for my family and other people.*

Once you have written a statement of purpose, review it daily for several weeks to verify that it accurately represents the purpose of your life.

2.   Set aside several hours to develop goals for yourself. Identify all the major goals you will need to accomplish in order to fulfill your purpose. You will probably come up with two to ten major goals. Take some time to review these life-long goals to make sure they seem worthwhile to you.

3.   Set aside an hour or more to break each of your life-long goals into specific long-term goals. Then break those down into smaller short-term goals. Finally, divide short-term goals into steps that can be accomplished by performing daily, weekly, and monthly disciplines. These activities will become your blueprint for success.

4.   Evaluate your goals. Determine how realistic they are, then determine which goals will require you to work with others in order to achieve them. Write down the goals that will require help, and begin developing a prospect list of people who could help with each goal. (Remember—try to select people who have similar goals and dreams.)

-chapter five-

The Successful Person Uses . . .
TIME MANAGEMENT

It has been my observation that most people get ahead during the time that others waste.

—*Henry Ford*

Most time is wasted, not in hours, but in minutes. A bucket with a small hole in the bottom gets just as empty as a bucket that is deliberately emptied.

—*Paul J. Meyer*

Imagine that your bank credited your account each morning with $86,400. Over the course of the day, you were free to use as much or as little of the money as you desired. You could use it any way you wanted—with just one condition. Whatever amount you failed to use by the end of the day could not be carried over to the next. And you could not save any of it for any reason. Whether you spent none or all of the previous day's amount, the next morning you would find another $86,400.

If you found yourself in such a situation, what would you do? If you are like most people, you would quickly figure out a way to spend that money each day. After purchasing everything you required for your immediate needs, you'd probably figure out a way to invest that money on a daily basis in order to get the greatest return in the long run.

THE CLOCK IS TICKING

Whether you know it or not, you face that situation every day of your life. Your "bank" is time, and you receive 86,400 seconds each day which you can spend any way you like. But if you fail to use those seconds, they are gone forever.

Successful people recognize the value of time. When inventor Thomas Edison was asked what he considered the most important item in the world, He responded, "time." Benjamin Franklin—inventor, author, and statesman—went even further when he said, "Dost thou love life? Then do not squander time, for that is the stuff life is made of."

If they stopped to think about it, most people would agree with Franklin. Life is comprised of the limited time we have on this earth. We consider life to be precious, yet we often squander time—the stuff that life is made of. Why does this happen? I believe there are several reasons:

1. People do not realize that the way they spend their time is something they can control. William A. Ward said, "We master our minutes, or we become slaves to them; we use time, or time uses us." The only difference between two individuals is not how much time they have—because we all have 24 hours in a day—but how that time is used.

> *The only difference between two*
> *individuals is not how*
> *much time they have, but how*
> *that time is used.*

2. They do not consider how little time we actually have to achieve success in life. Someone once estimated how the average American person who lives 72 years will spend his time:

   21 years sleeping,
   14 years working,
   7 years performing personal hygiene activities,
   6 years eating,
   6 years traveling,
   5 years waiting in line,
   4 years learning,
   3 years attending meetings,
   2 years returning calls,
   1 year searching for things lost,
   3 years in other activities.

If we expect to achieve success in our life, then we have very little time to do it–less than one fifth of our total time.

3. They don't realize how much time they waste. Many people have a very casual way of approaching the tasks they must accomplish each day. Their production is a fraction of their capacity.

4. They have neither system nor strategy for managing their time. By far the greatest reason for losing so much precious time is lack of planning. Charles C. Gibbons said, "One of the best ways to save time is to think and plan ahead; five minutes of thinking can often save an hour of work." If you value your time—and you must value time if you desire to succeed—you must plan your time.

THIEVES THAT STEAL TIME

One of the most important strategies for using your time wisely is to reduce drastically the time you waste. After all, you can't use what you've already lost. As Lord Chesterfield said, "I recommend to you to take care of the minutes; for [then the] hours will take care of themselves."

One of the most important strategies for using your time wisely is to drastically reduce the time you waste.

Here are ten top time-wasters. Control them, and you will increase the amount of time available to you each day:

1. LOOKING FOR THINGS THAT ARE LOST

Albert R. Karr reported in the *Wall Street Journal* that Accountemps, a temporary help agency, took a poll of 200 large-company executives. They discovered that executives waste over 10% of their time looking for misplaced items. *That means they are losing nearly six weeks out of every year!*

If you find yourself in this position, continually searching for items you've lost, the solution is to get organized. If you can, hire an efficient secretary, and pay him or her to organize things. But even if you can't hire someone, then devise systems of your own to keep from searching for everything.

One good rule of thumb is to throw away anything you don't need, and file everything you don't throw away. I have been filing information under simple subject headings for over thirty years, and I can place my hands on just about any piece of material I have in a matter of minutes.

2. LAZINESS

Time management is self-management. Many people have a difficult time getting themselves moving in a positive direction every day. For some, it's a motivation problem. For some, it's a discipline problem. Others simply have a temperament that causes them to lay back rather than move forward. Others have trouble keeping track of what they need to do and when they need to do it.

---

*Time management
is self-management.*

If laziness is a problem for you, use structure to succeed. Here are several suggestions:

A. Use a Planner. If you can't keep track of what you have to do and when you need to do it, use a tool that will help you record all of the information in an organized fashion in one place. Excellent tools are Franklin Planners, Day Timers, and Day Runners.

B. Work outside of the home. If you have trouble getting motivated, maybe you need a change of setting. Many people fall into a regular routine at home and have a hard time changing it. For others, home presents too many distractions; phone and doorbells ringing, interruptions from family and neighbors, television, radio, housework that needs doing, etc. Getting away may make it easier for you to focus. It may be the only step of discipline you need in order to work.

C. Start early. Nothing is as discouraging as suddenly realizing that you will not be able to finish a task because it is too late in the day to get started. When many people realize that they've run out of time, they write off the whole day and accomplish nothing. To avoid that tendency, practice to get an earlier start. You'll increase your options and be more assured of completing the day's goals. And if you get done early, you can stop for the day!

3. INTERRUPTIONS

According to Dr. Larry Baker, president of Time Management Center, Inc., interruptions are the greatest time wasters for executives. And interruptions not only waste time while they occur; they also force us to take time to refocus in order to continue where we left off.

Here are several ways to help avoid or minimize interruptions:

A. Hire an efficient secretary. One of the easiest ways to prevent interruptions is to put someone between you and the people who regularly interrupt you. If you control the times when people visit, you won't waste any time in getting refocused on a task. To be effective, however, you must provide other times when you are totally accessible so the people you work with don't feel excluded or resentful.

When you work in blocks of time you build momentum, and you are able to accomplish more work in a shorter period of time.

B. Learn to work in blocks of time. When you are involved in work that takes a lot of concentration, learn to work in large blocks—as many as four to six hours at a time. Do this for the same reason that you avoid interruptions: You'll avoid the need to refocus. In addition, when you work in blocks of time, you build momentum, and you are able to accomplish more work in a shorter period of time. You will have to make specific arrangements in order to get that much time to yourself. It won't just happen by itself. You may even have to find a special out-of-the-way place in order to work without being bothered.

C. Design your office to avoid distractions. If you can have any control over how your office is designed or built, make it so you have control over when you will see people. For example, don't set up your office so that people passing by can see you through a door or window and begin talking to you without an invitation. If you can, situate your office so that you can exit or go to the bathroom without having to see people. This way, whenever you do see people, you can be friendly and kind.

D. Change the way you use your telephone. Rather than using their telephones as helpful tools, many people become slaves to them. One of the ways to avoid this is to prevent your calls from ringing directly into your office. And set aside a particular time during the day to answer calls. Remember, your telephone is there for your convenience—not vice versa.

E. Learn to work early in the morning. I have found that I have fewer interruptions and distractions when I work early in the morning. If there is any way you can arrange to work early, you will find that it gives you a positive jump on the day, and it will increase your time available to work.

4. TRYING TO CARRY THE LOAD BY YOURSELF

The single greatest resource that each of us has to increase our productivity is other people. Despite this fact, many people try to carry the entire workload they have by themselves. The solution is delegation and empowerment.

The single greatest resource that each of us has to increase our productivity is other people.

Delegation is the ability to recognize the special abilities and limitations of others, combined with the ability to fit each person into the job where he or she will do best. Empowerment is the act of giving people what they need in order to accomplish their goals. When you can delegate to others, and empower them to succeed, everyone wins.

5. UNEXPECTED DELAYS OR TIME OPPORTUNITIES

How many times have you found yourself delayed unexpectedly with nothing to do? Once you get in that kind of position, there's little you can do but wait. It's one of the most frustrating—and time wasting—situations I know.

The only way to avoid situations like those is to plan ahead. Whenever I travel, I take work with me. When I'm flying, I don't get angry when there's an unexpected layover of an hour and a half. Instead, I open up my briefcase and I work. I never take a trip without taking a load of work with me—more than I could do if I had a dozen delays. I don't ever want to get caught empty-handed.

When I travel around town, I take work with me, too. My car has become a great "briefcase" full of resources. I always keep a book in the glove compartment, in case I'm stuck in traffic. I also use the tape deck, always carrying dozens of tapes in the car to listen to while I drive. In addition, my car always contains a mobile phone and small tape recorder. That way, I can return calls, dictate a letter, or record an idea that I might otherwise lose.

If you're prepared and make the best use of unexpected delays, you can turn lost time into productive time.

6. REGRETTING AND DAYDREAMING

I once saw an interesting picture that portrayed a busy street filled with fast-moving people and vehicles. Two men stood out from the crowd. On the left, an eager-faced man strode purposefully down the street, moving with the traffic. But on the right, oblivious to the hustle and bustle all around him, a stooped and depressed-looking man was moving in the opposite direction. And a caption under the picture described the man on the right. It said, "Looking for Yesterday."

Many people are like that stooped and beaten man. They expend energy thinking about the mistakes they've made or opportunities they've missed in the past. Or they daydream about the future. Both of these preoccupations are time wasters. Dag Hammarskjold said, "Do not look back and do not dream about the future. It will neither give you back the past nor satisfy your daydreams. Your duty, your reward—your destiny—are *here* and *now*."

Every moment you waste in preoccupation is a moment you steal from productivity. Learn from your mistakes, but quickly move on. And instead of daydreaming, work toward the fulfillment of your dreams and goals.

Every moment you waste in preoccupation is a moment you steal from productivity.

7. PROCRASTINATION

A friend asked a procrastinator how he ever got a day's work done. "That's simple," the procrastinator replied. "I pretend it is yesterday's work."

If you are a procrastinator, you are probably wasting much of your precious time. In the time that it takes most procrastinators to think about a task that must be done, worry about it, find an excuse to put it off, and then work through the guilt of having not done it, they could have already performed the task and moved on to the next activity.

There are several ways to deal effectively with procrastination:

A. Determine whether a given task must be done. Sometimes we procrastinate when we sense that a task is unimportant. If it is truly unimportant, rather than putting it off and then feeling guilty about it, eliminate it entirely. Getting rid of non-essential tasks is one of the keys to effective time management. Eliminate the clutter from your schedule.

B. Delegate tasks to others. Other times there are tasks that must be done, but that you may not enjoy doing. Sometimes your reluctance may be related to your personality type or talents. If you can delegate a necessary task to someone better suited to do it and who will enjoy doing it, then you both win.

C. Discover the benefits to get yourself moving. Procrastination often comes because we fail to see the benefit of doing an unpleasant task. In other words, the price we will have to pay by doing the task seems greater than the benefits we will receive from doing it. One of the best methods of dealing with this problem is to examine the task in light of your goals and vision. When it helps you move toward your goal, you'll find it easier to get motivated to do it.

D. Develop a discipline. For many people, procrastination has become a habit. For them, all the good reasons in the world to do a task may not be enough to break them out of that negative pattern. If this is your situation, you will have to retrain yourself and replace the bad habit of procrastination with good habits. Whenever you find yourself wanting to procrastinate, stop and determine what course of action you are going to take, and then ask yourself one more question: "When is the soonest I can get this done?" Give yourself a deadline, and stick to it. In time, you will begin changing your work pattern.

8. FAILING TO UNDERSTAND A PROBLEM

The opposite of procrastination is trying to solve a problem without enough information to do so. Out of a desire to find solutions quickly—ordinarily a very positive trait—some people act too quickly. Hastily-formed solutions can cause major problems if, while being implemented, they must be stopped and reversed in the face of new information.

If your natural inclination is to take control and "fix" things whether you understand the problem or not, you will need to discipline yourself in a way similar to that of the procrastinator. But instead of *forcing yourself to act by a given time,* you will need to *prevent yourself from acting before a given time.* This discipline will create enough time for you to receive the information you need to solve the problem effectively.

Emotional turmoil
can cause you to
lose energy and be less
productive.

---

9. PERSONAL NEGATIVE ATTITUDES

Emotional turmoil can cause you to lose energy and be less productive. Defensiveness, jealousy, strife, anger, and other negative emotions make it difficult to do your best, and you end up wasting time that could be spent productively.

If you have trouble with negative emotions, get help. If you have traumatic emotional issues from your past, work through them with a mental health professional. If you find yourself having a negative attitude, read positive books and listen to motivational tapes. Do whatever you can to cultivate a positive attitude.

10. FAILING TO KNOW AND LIST PRIORITIES

Even people who avoid most of the time-stealing problems listed above will not be as effective as they could be if they knew how to prioritize. The ability to know and list priorities is the most critical time management skill any person can acquire. In fact, it is so important that it deserves in-depth attention.

PRIORITIZE FOR POSITIVE RESULTS

French philosopher Blaise Pascal said, "The last thing one knows is what to put first." Unfortunately, for many people this is true. They don't have any idea how to rank the tasks and duties in their life in order of priority. They believe that activity means accomplishment, but nothing could be further from the truth.

Every act you perform has a corresponding value to you. That value is based on your talents, abilities, opportunities, vision, values, and goals. Let's say you and your neighbor both spend an hour performing the same task. For you it's the most valuable time you spend in a month. Yet he considers it a huge waste of time.

Let me give you an example: I know someone who is a wholesale sales manager for a particular type of automobile to dealerships in my area. He spends a large part of his time during the week visiting new managers of automobile dealerships with whom he does not yet do business. His goal is to cultivate positive relationships with those people, get to know their needs, and to inform them about the products that he sells.

The first time he visits a manager, he often spends the whole time conversing about subjects unrelated to his business. He focuses his energy on learning about the other person, on talking about his interests. They may talk about golf, for instance. If he is able to build a positive relationship, it could mean many sales during the years to come, and a substantial increase in his income. It would be an hour well spent.

On the other hand, if his neighbor, an architect who hates golf, were to go in and talk to that same manager for an hour, it could be torturous for him. It would neither help him in his business, nor would the conversation stimulate him.

This example may seem painfully obvious, but many people approach the tasks they do every day with absolutely no consideration for how much value they receive from performing them. To them, one task is much like another, and as long as the day gets filled with activity, they're happy. Or they may do the tasks that seem fun and ignore the ones that aren't as pleasant.

Successful people cannot manage their time using such an approach. They must employ a strategy of priorities to manage their time.

HOW TO DETERMINE YOUR PRIORITIES

Before you can determine what to do on a given day, you must first have a larger picture of how you should be spending your time. In order to do that, you need to ask yourself three questions:

1. What is required of me? Determining your priorities must always begin with what is required of you. There will always be certain duties and tasks that you must perform. One important thing to note is whether something required must be done, versus whether it must be done by you. There is a difference. Tasks that are necessary but need not be performed by you personally can be delegated and supervised.

A person should spend 80 percent of his time working in the area that gives him the highest return, and the remaining 20 percent in other areas.

---

2. What gives me the highest return? We should try to focus most of our time and energy on the things that give us the greatest return, tasks that we do better than anyone else. I generally use the Pareto (80/20) principle as a guideline in this area: a person should spend 80 percent of his time working in the area that gives him the highest return, and the remaining 20 percent in other areas. That is the most strategic use of time.

3. What gives me the greatest reward? For some people, the things that give the highest return also provide the greatest rewards in terms of personal satisfaction. But that is not always the case. No matter what your situation is, you need to spend time working in areas that reward you, that give you joy. Then you will be able to stay motivated because your work will continue to be fun.

HOW TO MAINTAIN YOUR PRIORITIES

Business and computer entrepreneur H. Ross Perot said, "Anything that is excellent or praiseworthy stands moment by moment on the cutting edge and must be constantly fought for." He understood that once you've determined your priorities, they don't just take care of themselves. You may have to fight to put them into practice, and you will certainly have to work hard to keep them in place. Here is a three-step plan that will help you to do that:

1. Evaluate. First evaluate your work according to its requirement, return, and reward for you.
2. Eliminate. Next, eliminate any tasks that you do not need to do. Delegate any tasks that must be done, but can be done by someone else. You might keep a file folder for every key person to whom you'd regularly delegate responsibilities. Then, as you identify tasks that you'd like to give them, place the items in their files. Whenever you see them, simply give them the contents of the file and explain the items that are not self-explanatory.
3. Estimate. Write down the tasks that must be done in order for you to accomplish your goals. Include information concerning how long it will take you to complete those tasks and who is available to help you succeed.

HOW TO ACT ON YOUR PRIORITIES

Once you have determined what should be done, you must act according to those priorities. Most people order their work according to the pressure they feel rather than the priorities they have. They are reactive instead of proactive. Successful people can't afford to work that way. Here are two suggestions that will help you work according to your priorities:

1. START EVERY DAY WITH A LIST OF YOUR PRIORITIES

Charles Schwab, president of Bethlehem Steel Company, granted an interview to an efficiency expert named Ivy Lee. In the interview, Lee stated that his firm could help Schwab do a better job of managing the company. Schwab agreed that he wasn't managing as well as he knew how. But what he needed wasn't more knowing, but more doing. He said, "We know what we should be doing; now if you can show us a better way of getting it done, I'll listen to you—and pay you anything within reason."

Lee said that he could share something in twenty minutes that would increase Schwab's company's achievements by at least 50 percent. Intrigued, and a little skeptical, Schwab asked Lee for the tip.

Ivy Lee handed Charles Schwab a blank sheet of paper. "Write down the six most important things you have to do tomorrow," he said. "Now number them in their order of importance to you and the company." That took about five minutes. "Now put the paper in your pocket, and first thing tomorrow morning, take it out and look at item number one," Lee continued. "Don't look at the others. Just focus on number one. Start working on it, and stay with it until it's completed. Then move on to number two and deal with it in the same way. Then number three, and so on, until you have to quit for the day. Don't worry if you have only finished one or two. You'll be working on the most important items."

"Do this every working day," Lee went on. "After you've convinced yourself of the value of this system, have your men try it. Try it as long as you like, and then send me your check for whatever you think the idea is worth."

The entire interview didn't take more than half an hour, but Schwab agreed to Lee's proposal. And in a few weeks Schwab sent Ivy Lee a check for $25,000. He stated that this simple lesson was the most profitable financially that he had ever learned in his life. The plan later received the credit for taking what was then a little-known steel company, and in five years turning it into the biggest independent steel producer in the world. It also helped make Charles Schwab a hundred million dollars.

People naturally resist doing their work in the order of its importance. Most would rather do what is pleasant or convenient. Yet nothing better manages a person's time than doing tasks by order of importance. Try it for a month and you will see amazing results. People will wonder where you got so much energy. But you haven't gained energy—you've simply learned to channel it in the best way you possibly can.

People naturally resist doing their work
in the order of its importance,
yet there is no single idea that better
manages a person's time.

2. WRITE OUR YOUR PRIORITIES AND
GIVE THEM A TIME SCHEDULE

Planning your day is critical to your success. It gives you a way to focus on what must be done on a moment-to-moment basis. But planning your week, month, or year is equally important. It gives you overall direction and keeps you focused on the bigger picture and the achievement of your goals.

Every month, I sit down with my calendar and a list of the main tasks I must accomplish during that month. Then I look for places in my calendar where I can plan to work on each of those tasks, and I schedule them accordingly.

The dividing line between success and
failure is often associated with how well a
person manages his time.

C. Neil Strait said, "The management of time should be the No. 1 priority for us. Without some organization of our day, it will waste away without purpose and drain away without accomplishment." It's very tempting to believe that a few minutes here or an hour there won't make much of a difference. But the dividing line between success and failure is often associated with how well a person manages his time.

Many times the difference is so subtle that we cannot see it until decades have passed. Other times the difference is obvious, as in the case of Alexander Graham Bell. When Bell was working on the telephone, another man, named Gray, was also trying to perfect the device. Both had their breakthrough at the same time. But Bell beat Gray to the patent office—by two hours. Neither man knew about the other, of course, but Bell became famous because of the difference of only 120 minutes.

The greatest possession you have is the 24 hours directly in front of you. Have you developed a strategy that will enable you to use it to the fullest?

SUCCESS STRATEGY ACTIVITIES

---

1. Set aside a block of time (possibly a Saturday) to clean and reorganize your office or work area. File everything you can, and throw or give away anything that you cannot file. Make a promise to yourself that in the future you will not go longer than two days without filing.

2. Look at the section on interruptions. Pick the area where you have the greatest problem and try the suggestion that is offered in that section for one month. Keep a record of all the extra work you get done as a result.

3. Set aside a couple of hours to answer the three questions to help you determine your priorities. Write down your answers, but avoid writing long detailed lists of duties. Instead, answer with a few statements for each question:

    a. What is required of me?
    b. What gives me the highest return?
    c. What gives me the greatest reward?

Once you've decided on your answers, type them up and post them somewhere in your work area to remind you to manage your time effectively.

4. For the next month, use the priority system that Ivy Lee taught to Charles Schwab. At the end of each day, write down the duties you must perform the following day. Then number them in order of their priority. The next day, work from your list, going from the most important task to the second most important, etc. At the end of the month, examine the effect of this new system on your productivity.

5. Set aside an hour or two to plan your month. Take your calendar and a list of all your responsibilities someplace where you will not be interrupted. Calculate the length of time each task will take, and put it on the calendar according to the blocks of time you have available. Don't forget to put them on the calendar according to their level of importance.

-chapter six-

The Successful Person Finds Ways to . . .
HANDLE STRESS

The punch that knocks you out is not so much the hard punch as the punch you didn't see coming.

—Joe Torres

If you can't fight and you can't flee, flow.

—Robert Eliot

One of the greatest problems faced by people today is stress. Even successful people who seem to have their lives in order are afflicted by stress-related problems. To show you how great a problem it has become in the United States in the last 100 years, all you need to know is that at the turn of the century, the top ten killers of people in the U.S. were all infectious diseases. In the 1990s, the top ten killers are all stress-related diseases.

SOME OBSERVATIONS ABOUT STRESS
We can't deal with something we don't understand, so any discussion of how to handle stress must begin with a few observations about stress.

ALL PEOPLE HAVE STRESS IN THEIR LIVES
When it comes to stress, the question is not, "Do you experience stress?" We all experience stress in some form or another. The question is, "What do you let affect you, and how does it affect you?"

Some kinds of stress can be avoided altogether through your mental attitude. But other forms are unavoidable, and you need to learn how to deal with them.

SOME KINDS OF STRESS CAN BE POSITIVE

It has been said that necessity is the mother of invention. In a similar way, stress can be called the mother of achievement. Sometimes stress brings out the best in people. It can prompt a person to find a better, smarter way of doing things. Maybe the word pressure or tension would better describe that kind of positive impetus.

---

*Stress causes some people to break,
and others to break records.*

You can see the positive effect of pressure particularly well in the lives of certain entertainers and athletes. Some actors, for instance, give their best performances when the pressure is on, when people important to them are in the audience. The same is true of some athletes. These are the big-game players whose level of play goes up during the championship game or the Olympic finals. Different people react differently to that kind of pressure. It causes some people to break, and others to break records.

MUCH STRESS IS UNNECESSARY

Most people worry unnecessarily about too many things. It's almost as though they search for things to give themselves stress. You may find that hard to believe, but if you have doubts, look at these figures about worry:

  40 percent of all things that people worry will happen never come to pass.
  30 percent of all worries involve past decisions that cannot be changed.
  12 percent focus on criticism from others who spoke because they felt inferior.
  10 percent are related to health, which worsens when a person worries.
  8 percent could be described as "legitimate" cause for concern.

Isn't that remarkable? Fewer than one stressor in ten should be a real cause for concern. All the others are things that we can learn to eliminate.

WHEN STRESS BECOMES STRAIN, IT'S HARMFUL

Sometimes stress can be a positive prompter and motivator, but it can also be destructive. In a study performed at Johns Hopkins Hospital in the United States, Dr. G. Canby Robinson discovered that out of 174 hospital patients studied, 140 were worriers. He also discovered that for over half of those 140 worriers, stress was the cause of their current physical symptoms.

Stress becomes strain when it is continuous. I've read that the human body reacts to stress in three stages: alarm, resistance, and exhaustion. He describes the stages as follows:

In the *alarm stage,* your body recognizes the stressor and prepares to fight or flee, by releasing some hormones from the endocrine glands. These hormones cause an increase in heartbeat and respiration, elevation in blood sugar level, increase in perspiration, dilated pupils, and slowed digestion. You then choose whether to use this burst of energy to fight or flee.

Stress becomes strain when it is continuous.

In the *resistance stage*, your body repairs any damage caused by the stress. But if the stressor hasn't gone away, the body cannot repair the damage and must remain alert.

This plunges you into the third stage—*exhaustion.* And if this state continues long enough, you could develop one of the "diseases of stress," like migraine headaches, heart irregularity, or even mental illness. Continued exposure to stress during the exhaustion stage causes the body to run out of energy, and may even stop bodily functions.

I believe that the best way to deal with stress is to avoid it or relieve it quickly.

PREVENTING STRESS FROM BECOMING DISTRESS

The bad news is that the world is filled with things that cause us stress. The good news is that we can learn to deal with it effectively. Here are eleven strategies to help handle stress successfully:

1. DEVELOP A PROPER PERSPECTIVE

One common characteristic of people who are able to avoid much of the stress that others experience is that they maintain a proper perspective regardless of life's circumstances. Earle Wilson called perspective, "The ability to see the present moment and immediate events against the background of a larger reference."

The bad news is that the world is filled with things that can cause us stress. The good news is that we can learn to deal with it effectively.

One of the best illustrations of perspective I've ever seen was something I read several years ago. It was a letter written by a college girl to her mother:

"Since I have been away at college one full semester, I think it's time that I bring you up to date concerning what is going on. Shortly after I arrived at college I got bored with dormitory life, and I stole $10 from my roommate's purse. With the money I rented a Honda motorcycle and crashed it into a telephone pole a few blocks from the college. I broke my leg, but I was rescued by the young medical student who lives upstairs in the apartment house at the corner.

He took me in, set my leg and nursed me back to good health. Thanks to him, I'm up and around again. We wanted to let you know that we're going to be married as soon as we clear up a problem with the blood test—it seems there is a disease that keeps showing up. But we do hope to be married before the baby arrives. Then we will be home shortly thereafter to live with you and Dad.

I know that you will love the baby as much as you love me, even though it will be of a different religion and race. And we'll only be staying with you until we get jobs, since my boyfriend had to drop out of medical school because of all the attention he was giving me in my condition. . . .

Okay. Really Mom—I didn't steal $10 from my roommate's purse, or rent a Honda motorcycle, or hit a telephone pole, or break my leg. I did not meet a young doctor, nor are we going to be married. There is no disease or test or baby to worry about. And I won't be home to live with you and Dad, and he won't be either.

However, I *am* getting a 'D' in geometry and an 'F' in geology, and I wanted you to accept these grades in their proper perspective."

There is no substitute for perspective. The next time you begin to feel stress because of minor difficulties, try to remember the bigger picture. It will help you to see things as they really are, instead of what you are afraid they might become.

2. STOP RUNNING FROM RISKS

As we've already discussed, fear of risk is a potential obstacle to success and a major cause of stress. Here is what Charles Swindoll has to say about risk:

"There are no absolute guarantees. No fail-safe plans. No perfectly reliable designs. No completely risk-free arrangements. Life refuses to be that neat and clean....

Running scared invariably blows up in one's face. All who fly risk crashing. All who walk risk stumbling. In short, all who live risk something.

To laugh is to risk appearing the fool. To weep is to risk appearing sentimental. To reach out for another is to risk involvement. To expose feelings is to risk exposing your true self. To love is to risk not being loved in return. To hope is to risk despair. To try is to risk failure.

Want to know the shortest route to ineffectiveness? Give in to stress and start running scared... Take no chances. Say no to courage and yes to caution. Expect the worst..."

Expect the best, and that's what
you'll most often get.

Worrying about risk truly is the shortest route to ineffectiveness. Since life is risk, we need to learn to stop running away from risk and face it optimistically. Expect the worst, and that's what you will get every time. Expect the best, and that's what you'll most often get.

3. WORK IN YOUR AREAS OF STRENGTH

People who work in their areas of strength are less likely to become victims of stress, even when they make mistakes. For a good example of this, look at former American football quarterback Roger Staubach. When playing for the Dallas Cowboys, he was once asked what his reaction was when a pass he threw was intercepted by someone on the other team. He replied, "When I throw one [an interception] I can't wait to get my hands on that football. I can't wait to throw another pass."

Because he was so good at playing football, Staubach's response to adversity was not stress, but a stronger desire to continue playing. That is a common response from people who work in their areas of strength.

If you aren't sure of your areas of strength, here's a way to identify them: If your mistakes challenge you instead of causing stress, then you're probably working in an area of strength. If every mistake makes you feel threatened and tense, you are probably working in an area of weakness.

4. AVOID THE RAT RACE

In recent years, some people have called the competitive business world in the United States the "rat race." In this intense, almost irrationally competitive struggle between people in an industry, players compete fiercely against one another, even "keeping score" in terms of the amount of personal gain and wealth they acquire. Concerning the rat race, comedian Lily Tomlin said, "The trouble with the rat race is that even if you win, you're still a rat."

When a person enters the rat race of competition, he often loses sight of working toward his goals in order to achieve his vision. Anyone who does this is subjecting himself to unnecessary stress, because no matter how hard he works, he can't be satisfied. What he's defined as "success" is unattainable, because he's competing in too many areas. He'll never "win." A writer for *The Herkimer Citizen* suggested that we could learn something from the animals when he wrote,

> "So far as is known, no bird ever tried to build more nests than its neighbor; no fox ever fretted because he had only one hole in which to hide; no squirrel ever died of anxiety lest he should

not lay by enough nuts for two winters instead of one; and no dog ever lost any sleep over the fact that he did not have enough bones laid aside for his declining years."

Work hard. Strive to achieve your goals. But don't do it to the detriment of your family, your health or your fellow man. Nothing is worth that kind of sacrifice or the stress that comes with it.

5. GET OFF THE ROAD OF OVERLOAD

Many of us are like the farmer who stood in the middle of his field and said, "I don't go to work; I'm surrounded by it." We keep taking on more responsibilities until we can't possibly fulfill them all competently. And that causes stress.

Sometimes you have to give up what is merely good in order to do what is best.

Many of us need to stop taking on more work. If you are a person who loves to try new things, you might be susceptible to overload. Stop periodically and remind yourself that no one can do everything and still do what is important effectively. Sometimes you have to give up what is merely good in order to do what is best.

6. DEVELOP STRONG CONVICTIONS

Dr. Harold Dodds said, "It's not the fast tempo of life that kills, but the boredom. It is the feeling that nothing is worthwhile that makes men ill and unhappy." Lack of purpose and direction seems to be epidemic in the twentieth century. People no longer know what they believe. So many have replaced values with doubts—and conviction with apathy.

German philosopher Friedrich Nietzsche described our need for convictions in this way: "If we have a *why* we shall get along with almost any *how*." Convictions enable us to face nearly any situation in life with courage and dignity. And the deeper the convictions, the stronger a person is—and the less likely to experience stress in the face of adversity.

Every truly successful person I know has strong personal convictions. I even credit my own success in life to my convictions—

my belief in God and the plan He has for my life. That belief has been my motivation and the source of my strength, helping me to remain positive and relatively stress-free in the midst of life's circumstances.

7. GIVE UP YOUR RIGHTS

The United States was founded on the premise that all people have certain inalienable rights. Now that's a wonderful idea, but in recent years, it's been overused. Many Americans have become obsessed with fighting for their *rights*—to the neglect of their *responsibilities.*

One of the problems with fighting for your rights is that it causes a great amount of stress and emotional fatigue. You won't always be able to get everything you want or are "entitled to," no matter how hard you try. All this preoccupation with your rights will do is cultivate five very destructive emotions: resentment, bitterness, anger, hatred, and fear.

You've probably heard the statement:"It is better to give than to receive." Anyone who has ever given a gift to a child knows that statement is true. But the same can be true when it comes to your rights. We can find peace simply by not always demanding to have our way. Giving up your rights can bring great joy and greatly reduce stress.

8. REPROGRAM YOUR MIND

Most of what we experience emotionally is a result of the way we think. Stress is no exception. The amount of stress we experience is directly related to our outlook. And our thoughts are directly related to what we put into our minds.

Most of what we experience emotionally is a result of the way we think.

Computer experts know that the output you receive from a computer is the result of the input it gets. The same is true with our brains. Our output—what we say, think, and do—is generated by our input—what we read, watch, hear, and see. We each can choose our input from one of two categories: things that add either *stress* or *stability* to our lives.

For example, I know a lot of people who are fearful of others. They won't walk in their own neighborhoods after dark. They put bars on their windows and extra locks on their doors. Yet most of them have never had any traumatic problems of their own. They are afraid because of input that they allow into their minds—all the negative things on television. This input causes them to live stress-filled lives.

Be aware that your mind is constantly undergoing programming. And you are the only one who can choose what your mind will receive. Stay away from things that are negative and build stress. Instead, follow the advice of Paul the apostle, who said in Philippians 4:8, "Whatever is true, whatever is noble, whatever is right, whatever is pure, whatever is lovely, whatever is admirable— if anything is excellent or praiseworthy—think about such things."

9. TURN YOUR FOCUS OUTWARD

As I mentioned in chapter two, people who focus too much on themselves are often discouraged. As a result, they experience stress. If you find yourself becoming preoccupied with your own concerns, spend time helping others. In helping others, we often heal ourselves.

10. HAVE SOMEONE TO TALK TO

Much of the stress that we experience occurs because we bottle up our feelings instead of expressing them. And according to many doctors, a person who continually stuffs his emotions instead of letting them out is a prime candidate for a heart attack.

To avoid that kind of stress, develop a few close relationships, where you can talk about both positive and negative things. Be sure it is someone with whom you can be totally honest. He or she should not judge you or ever use what you say against you.

11. FIND AN ACTIVE WAY TO RELEASE STRESS

All of us do things to reduce the stress in our lives. Some of them are healthy and positive, and some of them aren't. For example, some of us reduce stress by eating. Unfortunately, when we use this method to reduce our stress, we then need to find a way to *reduce our weight!*

Healthier ways to reduce stress include playing golf or hitting tennis balls. If you can name one person who really contributes to your stress, simply write his name on the ball and give it a good "whack!" That will definitely make you feel better. Other people run or take long walks. What you choose to do isn't as important as just doing it. Pick something that you really enjoy doing, and have some fun.

Stress can't usually be blamed on having too much to do. Instead, it usually results from the way you *think* about what you are doing and what is happening to you. The bottom line is that your ability to survive stress is based on how you handle it. As Alexis Carrel said, "People who don't know how to fight worry die young."

Expect stress—because it will come. Work on changing your thinking and habits. Whenever possible, avoid stress. But when you can't avoid it, use healthy strategies to handle it. Don't allow stress to be the unexpected punch that knocks you out—and keeps you from achieving success.

SUCCESS STRATEGY ACTIVITIES

1. The next time life's day-to-day problems bother you and start to cause stress, do something to change your perspective. Do volunteer work. Arrange to visit terminally ill people in the hospital, take toys to an orphanage, feed the homeless, or visit people in a nursing home. Get out and help others, and see what happens. After you overcome your initial fear or reluctance, you will find that your perspective has improved. Your problems will not seem as big to you.

2. This activity has two parts:
    a. Ask a close friend or your spouse to help you discover your areas of strength and weakness. First, write down five tasks that you perform on a regular basis that make you feel nervous, dis-

couraged, or threatened. Then write down five tasks that make you feel encouraged, challenged, or confident. Ask your spouse or friend to create a similar list for you, based on their observations. Then compare lists. Be open-minded, and don't get defensive if the person identifies areas of weakness that you didn't expect. Your goal is to discover or verify your weaknesses and strengths.

b. Based on the strengths and weaknesses that you identified, create a plan which would help you to start spending more of your work time in areas of strength and remove you from your areas of weakness.

3. Set aside an hour or two to identify, define, and write out your convictions. You might have a few or a dozen. Begin by making a broad list of all your major beliefs. Then narrow those down into specific convictions. Here's one good way to know the difference between the two: a conviction is a belief you would be willing to die for.

4. Spend one week keeping careful track of what you are currently putting into your mind. Write down in a small notebook what you are hearing, seeing, and reading, along with the amount of time spent in each activity. Record the names of the songs you listen to, the television programs you watch, the conversations you participate in, the books and articles you read, etc. Then at the end of the week, note next to each entry whether it had a positive or negative influence. Don't list anything as neutral; even music without lyrics has an emotional effect. Finally, calculate the percentages. Are you filling yourself with enough positive material to counter the negative?

5. If you don't already have an active method for reducing stress, try to find one this week. Try going for a long walk; playing racquetball, tennis, or golf; running; chopping wood; playing darts— anything as long as it is active, takes energy, and is fun. Once you've discovered an activity or activities, plan your schedule for the next two months so that you can practice that activity at least once a week.

-chapter seven-

The Successful Person Values . . .

RELATIONSHIPS

The most important single ingredient to the formula of success is knowing how to get along with people.

—Theodore Roosevelt

I will pay more for the ability to deal with people than any other ability under the sun.

— John D. Rockefeller

SUCCESS MEANS INCLUDING OTHERS

I recently read about a survey that a group of teachers sent to more than 2,000 employers as a service to their students. They asked the employers, "For the last three persons dismissed from your business, can you give one reason why you let them go?" The one overwhelming response surprised the teachers. In two out of three cases listed by respondents, regardless of the type of work or area of the country, the answer was the same: They were dismissed because they couldn't get along with other people.

---

*Relationships either make us
or break us.*

Business people who accomplish great things recognize the importance of people to their success. A.H. Smith, former president of a leading railroad in the United States, said, "A railroad is 95 percent man and 5 percent iron." His observation reflects what various scientific studies have shown. If you learn how to deal with others, you will have traveled about 85% of the road to success in any business. And you will have gone about 99% of the way toward personal happiness.

The bottom line is that relationships either make or break us. First, each relationship affects others. The quality of my relationship with my spouse affects my relationships with my children. And my family relationships set the tone for my interaction at work. And the quality of our relationships with coworkers, bosses, and employees are largely responsible for our success or failure in business. All the technical expertise and skills in the world will not enable a person to achieve what he wants unless he can develop positive relationships with others.

If you have doubts about this, consider these facts. In actual studies of leadership in American business, it's been proven that ...

1. The average executive spends three-fourths of his working day dealing with ... people.
2. The largest single cost in most businesses is ... people.
3. The biggest and most valuable asset any company has is its ... people.
4. All plans by an executive are carried out by—or fail to be carried out by ... people.

If you want to be a success in life, no matter what goals you have or profession you choose, you must learn to develop positive relationships with people.

HOW TO BUILD GOOD RELATIONSHIPS WITH PEOPLE

The ability to develop good relationships with others doesn't need to be a mystery. Good people skills are not restricted to those born with some magical ability, although some are born with exceptionally good instincts in this area. For most of us, the skills necessary to develop good relationships are learned. Use these fifteen guidelines to build good relationships with others:

1. TAKE YOUR FOCUS OFF YOURSELF

The first step each person needs to take in order to build positive relationships is to take his eyes off of himself. People who think primarily of themselves when interacting with others rarely build positive lasting relationships. The potential for good relationships increases dramatically when you begin focusing on others.

2. CARE A LOT ABOUT THEM

One of the keys to relationships—and to success in all of life—is expressed in one of my favorite statements by my friend John Maxwell: "People don't care how much you know until they know how much you care." All the skill, talent, and education in the world will never impress another person more than your genuine, heartfelt care for them. This is especially important when you are in a position of authority over someone. If you don't first establish that you care, your positive influence over them will be very limited.

All the skill, talent, and education in the world will never impress another person more than your genuine, heartfelt care for them.

Statistics back up this concept. The *Wall Street Journal* recently published a study by a research firm named Teleometrics International, which surveyed 16,000 executives in a variety of fields. The top thirteen percent of respondents, who were identified as "high achievers," stated that they cared as much about people as they did about profits.

3. KNOW A LOT ABOUT THEM

Few things have a more positive effect on others than finding out and remembering things about them. Knowing a lot about people is a positive sign that you care, and it creates a positive, lasting bond.

An excellent example of this from history can be seen in the career of the French general and emperor, Napoleon Bonaparte. This military leader was as strategic in his interaction with his men as he was on the battlefield. He knew every officer in his army, and he liked to wander through the camp, greeting each officer by name. He then made sure to talk about a maneuver in which he knew this officer had been involved. He never missed an opportunity to inquire about any soldier's hometown, wife and family. And it always amazed the man to see how much detailed personal information about him his emperor knew.

Since every officer felt Napoleon's personal interest in him—proven by his comments and questions—it is easy to understand the devotion they all felt for him.

4. DON'T UNDERESTIMATE THE VALUE OF ANY INDIVIDUAL WITH WHOM YOU DEAL

I once heard a story about a young politician's first campaign speech. He was very eager to make an impression, but when he entered the auditorium, he found only one man in the audience. He waited for awhile, hoping more people would show up. But none did. Finally he said to the one man in the audience, "Look, I'm just a young politician starting out. Do you think I ought to deliver this speech or dismiss the meeting?" The man thought for a moment and replied, "Sir, I am just a cowhand. All I know is cows. Of course, I do know that if I took a load of hay down to the pasture and only one cow came up, I'd still feed it."

Meet each person with positive
anticipation, and expect every encounter
to yield positive results.

Many of us think in the same way as that young politician. We desire to have a great influence, but we associate influence with numbers. Actually, we can have the greatest impact on those we meet *one at a time.*

Meet each person with positive anticipation, and expect every encounter to yield positive results. Treat everyone as important, even the people you come in contact with every day. Don't miss the important opportunities that are right under your nose.

5. DON'T TAKE ADVANTAGE OF PEOPLE

One of the things I hate is seeing people trying to advance themselves at the expense of others. Besides being wrong, it simply doesn't work. Advancing yourself by taking advantage of others gives only the illusion of success. In the long run it hurts you as well as those around you.

Advancing yourself
by taking advantage of others gives
only the illusion of success.

Achieving success takes time. It's a process, and must include other people to work effectively. Whenever a person takes advantage of someone else, he's trying to take a shortcut. And this hurts his chances for the future by decreasing his opportunities, along with the number of people who are willing to help him along his way. Shortcuts to success end up being lengthy detours. If you try enough "shortcuts," you may never reach your destination at all. As U.S. President Dwight D. Eisenhower said, "There are no victories at bargain prices."

6. ASK FOR ADVICE OR FAVORS

One of the best ways to build positive relationships with others may come as a surprise: ask for help. Most of us love the opportunity to show our expertise by giving our advice on a subject. And knowing someone needs our help often provides a feeling of authority or strength.

Ben Franklin was a talented diplomat, and he used this practice to convert an enemy into a life-long friend. In 1736, Franklin's name was on the list of candidates for Clerk of the General Assembly. He felt confident of the nomination in many ways. But one very powerful and influential man was strongly opposed to him. Franklin knew he must win this man's friendship or lose.

"Having heard that he had in his library a certain very scarce book," Franklin stated of this man in his autobiography, "I wrote a note to him, expressing my desire of perusing that book and requesting he would do me the favor of lending it to me." The enemy, flattered by the request, loaned Franklin the book. And as a result, he became one of his most ardent supporters.

7. ALWAYS "BRING SOMETHING TO THE TABLE"

Asking someone else to help you is an excellent way to start or repair a relationship. But to remain positive and healthy, all relationships must be mutually beneficial. One person cannot continually receive while giving little or nothing in return. The best relationships are those in which both parties are constantly receiving from one another. So if you desire to make your relationships positive, always make an effort to bring something positive "to the table" when you get together.

The best relationships are those in which both parties are constantly receiving from one another.

Why do you spend time with friends or colleagues? Although meeting solely for the exchange of personal information and pleasantries is fine, your meetings can be especially rewarding if you "bring something" for the other person. Bring positive things like ideas, business opportunities, material for personal growth or encouragement. Almost anything that benefits the other person or helps her with her goals can build and strengthen your relationship and help both of you to grow.

8. BE CONSIDERATE OF PEOPLE'S FEELINGS

People are emotional beings. Despite our desire to be rational and logical, we can never escape our emotional reactions. If you want to be successful in your relationships, be considerate of the feelings of others. Dr. Paul Parker points out, "You can handle people more successfully by enlisting their feelings than by consulting their reason."

I once heard about a woman who went into a shoe store to buy a new pair of shoes. The salesman obligingly did everything he could to fit her, but without success. At last he told her, "Lady, I just can't fit you. One of your feet is larger than the other."

Naturally, this infuriated the woman, and she got up to leave. But the store manager, who had overheard the conversation, stopped her. The salesman watched in bewilderment as the manager gently persuaded the customer to sit down again. After only a few minutes of measuring and fitting, the manager sold her a pair of shoes.

"How in the world did you do that?" the salesman asked after the woman had gone. "Her feet are still different sizes. Didn't you have to tell her the same thing I did?"

"Not quite," explained the manager, "I told her that one of her feet was smaller than the other."

The manager told the customer the truth, yet he considered her feelings and approached her with tact and respect. In this way, he succeeded in seeing the situation through her eyes.

There is great power in the ability to discern and then respectfully consider other people's feelings. As novelist Joseph Conrad said, "Give me the right word and the right accent, and I will move the world."

9. BE ALERT TO PROVIDE SERVICE TO OTHERS

The development of positive relationships is only one of the benefits of serving others. But it has a huge impact. People are naturally drawn to others who help them, and most of us desire to return kindness with kindness. If you look for opportunities to provide service to others, you will live a more satisfying life and develop many good relationships.

Another practical side of providing service is that in our competitive business world, good service is often the only quality that separates one company from another. As the Nordstrom department stores in the western United States say, "The only difference between stores is the way they treat their customers."

Look at the following reasons why different customers stop using a business:

1% die;
3% move away;
5% leave because of other friendships;
9% leave for competitive reasons (usually price);
14% leave because of product dissatisfaction;
68% leave because of an attitude of indifference toward them by an employee.

Isn't that last statistic remarkable? Two out of every three customers that you lose leave because they are dissatisfied with the service they receive. Thus, the single greatest positive thing you can do for your business is to improve the service you provide. Positive service helps build positive relationships.

Two out of three customers
that you lose leave because
they are dissatisfied with the service
they receive.

10. BE A GOOD LISTENER

It is a common characteristic of people who are especially good at building relationships that they listen attentively when someone else talks. After all, do you know anyone who doesn't enjoy talking with a good listener?

A key to becoming a good listener is learning to encourage the other person to talk about himself. Usually all it takes is a couple of well-directed questions. If you are kind but persistent, you can even persuade the most untalkative person to talk about himself. As a result, you learn more about who he is and how your relationship can grow, and he learns that what he says really matters to you.

11. TALK ABOUT THE OTHER PERSON'S INTERESTS

One of the most common mistakes some people make when initiating a relationship is trying to interest the other person in themselves. They try talking about one interest or desire after another in the hopes of hitting on a subject that the other person will find interesting. But they're going about things backwards.

When initiating a relationship
it is a good strategy to focus your attention
on the other person's interests.

A better strategy is to focus on other persons' interests. When you do this, you avoid wasting time guessing at what they might enjoy, and you demonstrate your interest in who they are. This gives them a positive feeling about you, and establishes a connection more quickly than any other method.

If you're perceptive, you can usually learn about another person's interests almost immediately. When in someone's home or office, look at the pictures, trophies, mementos or books they have on display. Something will catch your eye. If their interest is new to you, you can take the opportunity to learn from the conversation. And if it's an area where your interests already lie, you will enjoy the conversation twice as much.

12. MAKE THE OTHER PERSON FEEL IMPORTANT
In chapter one, I mentioned that treating others well and making them feel important is a part of being a positive thinker. It's important to remind yourself that there is nothing on earth more important than people. And it costs us nothing to give another person praise and respect and make him feel important.

13. BE CREDIBLE AND CONSISTENT
Few things can damage a friendship more quickly or severely than when we break a trust. This can occur in a broken promise, or just inconsistency in daily life.

People must first buy into you
before they will buy into your vision
or your product.

Lost credibility not only damages friendships, it also destroys business relationships. People must first buy into you before they will buy into your vision or product. Opportunities disappear quickly when others cannot count on you.

14. AVOID ARGUMENTS
Discussion between people is healthy and positive. Arguments, on the other hand, are never good. What's the difference? Arguments are the forceful attempt to change another person's point of view. They always result in one person "winning" and the other "losing." But discussion is the interchange of ideas with the goal of settling on the best solution for everyone. It is the attempt to create a win-win situation.

Arguments always cause some kind of damage. Even if you "win," you lose something in your relationship with the other person. The next time you and someone else have differing points of view on something, follow these guidelines in order to resolve the disagreement while building the relationship:

A. Welcome the disagreement. Have you ever heard the statement, "When two partners always agree, one of them is not necessary"? If the other person brings up something that you haven't thought about, be thankful that it's brought to your attention. Perhaps this disagreement is your chance to be corrected before you make a serious mistake.

B. Distrust your first reaction to defend yourself. Our first natural inclination in a disagreeable situation is to be defensive. But be careful. Whenever you become defensive and begin justifying yourself, you often make it very difficult to change your position later. You will also prevent yourself from benefitting from the other person's ideas. Keep calm and focus on learning, not proving you were "right."

C. Control your temper. Getting angry always makes communication harder, not easier. Remember, you can measure the size of a man by what makes him angry. So take a deep breath and try to remain objective.

D. Listen first. Give your opponent a chance to talk. Let him finish. Do not resist, defend, or debate, or you'll build barriers to communication. Instead, try to build bridges of understanding.

E. Look for areas of agreement. When you have heard the other person out, dwell first on the areas where you agree. This builds rapport and common ground, where you can build a solution that's good for both of you. And try to be agreeable and flexible when possible. As Thomas Jefferson said, "In matters of principle, stand like a rock; in matters of taste, swim with the current."

F. Be honest. Look for areas where you can admit error, then express them. Apologize for your mistakes. This is not only the right thing to do; it also serves to disarm the other person and reduce his defensiveness. And it provides a graceful way to move toward your ultimate goal—a positive solution for both of you.

G. Promise to think over and carefully study his ideas. When you tell your opponent that you'll consider his point of view, really mean it. He may be right. And you don't want to ignore his ideas, have trouble as a result, and then later hear him say, "I tried to tell him, but he wouldn't listen."

H. Thank him sincerely for his interest. Anyone who takes the time to disagree with you is interested in the same things you are. See him as someone who really wants to help, and he can turn out to be a friend.

I. Postpone action to provide time to think through the problem. Suggest that a new meeting be held later that day or the next day when all the facts are in. Then in preparation for this meeting ask yourself some hard questions and think through both perspectives.

Remember, the goal of discussion is to find a mutually beneficial solution, not to convince the other person that you're "right." But occasionally, you might need to encourage someone to change his point of view. If that occurs, remember that while the better part of wisdom is to admit when you are wrong, you should never demand it from others. Always approach these situations with tact and caution.

First, provide an "escape-hatch" so the other person doesn't feel resentful if he finds he really ought to change his position. Present your case, explaining that you held his opinion until: you discovered the information you are presenting; someone else showed you a better way; or the situation was presented to you in a new light. Communicate that intelligent people can change their minds and still retain their dignity.

Second, whenever possible, help him believe that he thought of the idea. Find common ground in your arguments, and repeat any of his remarks that are consistent with your point. Bring up any evidence that you know he already believes. Tell how it is consistent with his experience, and how conditions now favor shifting position even though they may not have in the past.

Finally, let the person convince himself if possible. And never claim credit for changing his mind. That can change him from feeling like you are both winners to feeling like you won at his expense.

15. BECOME A STUDENT OF PEOPLE

To develop positive relationships with others, you must understand people—to know their fears, hopes, and dreams. To learn to understand others, become a student of humanity. Talk with people. Listen to their dreams. Watch them. Learn how they think. Reading books and listening to tapes can certainly help, but don't forget to spend time with people yourself and learn about them. You must develop a lifestyle, not an academic study.

Joe McCarthy, the manager of the New York Yankees during some of their best years, was an outstanding student of people. He once interviewed a coach to consider bringing him up to the Yankees baseball team from one of their farm teams.

McCarthy wasn't sure about this young, inexperienced guy. He didn't look like he could handle the players. So Joe asked, "How much do you know about psychology?"

The coach said he had studied it in college. "So you think you're good," said McCarthy, still doubtful. The coach replied: "I don't know how good I am, but it's a subject I've studied."

"All right," McCarthy said, "I'll give you a test." Then McCarthy told the younger coach a story about a situation he'd faced a few years before.

"A few years ago, I approached my shortstop, Frankie Crosetti, looking for help solving a problem. 'Frank,' I said, 'I'm not satisfied with the way Lou Gehrig is playing first base. He's too lackadaisical, so I want you to help me. From now on, charge every ground ball. Then fire it as quickly and as hard as you can to first base. Knock Gehrig off the bag if you can. I don't care if you throw wild or not, but throw it fast and make it tough for him.'"

McCarthy then turned to the new coach and said, "Now, that's the story. What conclusions would you draw from it?"

The young man considered the matter for a minute, then answered, "I guess you were trying to wake up Gehrig."

"See?" McCarthy shrugged his shoulders in resignation. "You missed the point entirely. There wasn't a thing wrong with Gehrig. Crosetti was the one who was sleeping. I wanted to wake up Crosetti."

———————

The successful person knows the value of good relationships. His ability to achieve his goals and carry out his vision is largely dependent on the people around him. He simply cannot do everything alone. Nor does he want to even if he could.

Even the most shy or abrasive person can change and learn to cultivate positive relationships. One of my favorite examples from history of someone who grew in this area is Benjamin Franklin. At the time of the American Revolutionary War, he was an amazingly successful people-person. He convinced his countrymen to improve lighting and paving in Philadelphia, and to establish the nation's first fire company, the first free library, the American Philosophical Society, the academy which eventually became the University of Pennsylvania, America's first public hospital, and many other institutions and practices. In addition, he convinced France to give the colonies the help they needed to win the war against England.

Even the most shy or abrasive person can change and learn to cultivate positive relationships.

Franklin was a powerful influencer, but he hadn't always been that way. In his youth, he was dogmatic and offensive, until one day a Quaker friend took him aside and gave him a lecture on human relations. Afterward, Franklin said, "I made it a rule to forebear all direct contradiction to the sentiments of others, and all positive assertion of my own." He began using expressions such as "I imagine" and "it appears to me" instead of "certainly" or "undoubtedly." And he listened open-mindedly to the other person's point of view. Due to these changes, he said, he had so much influence in public affairs.

He also played down his own importance. When Franklin wanted to establish an academy of learning, he didn't try to get others to rally around "his idea." He promoted the project as a group effort of "some public-spirited gentlemen." He always avoided "presenting myself to the public as the author of any scheme for their benefit."

Franklin really did understand people. When he was in charge of the defense of the northwestern frontier of Pennsylvania, he had a chaplain who complained that the men did not attend prayer meetings regularly. Many military officers during Franklin's time punished men for non-attendance. But not him. Instead, he suggested that the chaplain take charge of doling out the daily ration of rum and make it available to the men only immediately after the daily prayer service. "Never," said Franklin, "were prayers more generally and more punctually attended."

If you aren't naturally gifted at developing relationships, don't despair. Like Benjamin Franklin, you can grow in this area. Work at improving your skills.

If you already have a talent for working with others, keep fine tuning your abilities. You can never be too effective relationally. Your success is nearly limitless.

SUCCESS STRATEGY ACTIVITIES

---

1. Pick one person each week to get to know better. It can be someone with whom you work, socialize or go to church. Take time to talk with that person. Encourage him to tell you about himself. Then do whatever it takes to remember the information. When you later see that person, ask heart-felt questions based on your knowledge of him.

2. Set aside some time to reflect on whether you are advancing yourself by taking advantage of others. If you are, go to the person you have exploited, and try to repair the relationship: apologize, offer restitution, change your interaction so that it is mutually beneficial and determine not to repeat the same error.

3. Select someone you want to know or with whom you'd like to develop a business relationship. Try initiating a relationship with that person through one of the following strategies:
    a. Ask the person for advice.
    b. Ask the person to do you a favor.
    c. Learn what the person's interests are and find out something about him or her. Then meet with the person with the goal of discussing only those interests.

4. The next time you plan to meet with a friend or colleague, "bring something to the table." Ahead of time, buy a book or tape that you know he will enjoy. Plan to introduce him to a good business or personal contact of yours. Be creative and work to help him achieve his goals.

5. Become a student of people by creating a "People Notebook." At the end of each day, try to record one observation either about a specific person you encountered during the day, or about people in general based on your experiences. In addition, write down insightful quotes that you hear or read about people. Then at the end of each month, review your notes and quotes. Look for patterns, and draw truths about people from them. Then file especially good quotes for later use. Review the notebook again at the end of the year.

-chapter eight-

The Successful Person Develops . . .

COMMUNICATION SKILLS

The great challenge in communicating is to understand the mind, the background, and the thinking process of your audience. If you know these, you can prevent a lot of "communication static."

—*Wayne Pennington*

Give every man thine ear, but few thy voice.

—*William Shakespeare (Hamlet)*

In the previous chapter I explained that true success cannot be achieved without relationships with other people. But how meaningful and deep those relationships can be is determined by communication. Because of this, the success of your marriage, job, and other relationships depends a great deal on your ability to communicate.

The success of your marriage, job, and relationships with others depends a great deal on your ability to communicate.

COMMUNICATION BASICS

Webster's *New World Dictionary of the English Language* defines the word communication as the "giving or exchanging of information, signals, or messages by talk, gestures, or writing." That definition characterizes communication as a one-sided process. But it's not. Communication involves interaction between two people. For it to be effective, both participants must be constantly giving and receiving information, both verbally and non-verbally. Let me give

111

you an example of what can happen when communication doesn't flow in both directions between people. At the Bell Telephone Laboratories in the United States, a scientist conducted the following experiment: First, he divided the participants into three groups. Then he paired up every member of each group, and gave them the task of attempting to communicate with each other. Person A in each pair was given a set of dominoes that were arranged in a specific pattern. Then Person B was given identical dominoes that were scattered across a table. Person A's goal was to tell Person B how to arrange his dominoes so that both sets matched. But the pairs in each group had certain restrictions:

Group 1: All the A's could talk to the B's, but the B's were not allowed to respond. At the end of the experiment, none of the B's in this group had the pattern right.
Group 2: The B's still couldn't talk back to the A's, but they could press a buzzer and ask the A's to repeat their instructions. At the end of the experiment, some of the B's in this group had the correct pattern.
Group 3: The A's and the B's could talk to one another freely in full two-way communication. When the experiment was finished, every single B had the pattern right.

Every time two people attempt to communicate, many things can happen. Here are several of the possible messages that can be sent when one person speaks to another:

1. What the speaker intends to say.
2. What the speaker actually says.
3. What the speaker is understood to have said.
4. What the hearer wants to hear.
5. What the hearer actually hears.

All of these possibilities exist with every utterance we speak. Obviously, the possibility of misunderstanding is tremendous.

To make things even more interesting, as he listens, the hearer is also sending verbal and non-verbal messages back to the speaker. These in turn can be correctly understood, misunderstood, or ignored. It can be a very complicated process.

General Ulysses S. Grant, the American Civil War hero who later became President of the United States, understood how easily an attempt at communication can be misunderstood. He kept a particularly simple-minded soldier just outside his office at all times. Before issuing any order, he read it to this young fellow. If that soldier understood it, the general sent it. If not, Grant returned to his desk to simplify or clarify it.

DEVELOP POSITIVE ONE-ON-ONE COMMUNICATION SKILLS

Some people have a natural talent for communication. They seem able to communicate effectively just about anything to nearly anyone. For others, miscommunication seems to be the norm rather than the exception. No matter what your communication skill level is, it can be improved. Use the following guidelines to learn (or remind yourself of) some important things to keep in mind when you try to communicate with another person:

STOP TALKING!

The most common communication difficulty that people experience is not keeping quiet long enough to let the other person talk. And you cannot listen if you are talking all the time. God gave us two ears, but only one mouth. He did that for a reason.

If you find that you regularly do more than half of the talking in your conversations, you are probably talking too much. And if you are in a service or sales profession, you should be doing much less than 50% of the talking. As mentioned in the previous chapter, you should try to focus on the other person's interests and needs.

Spending most of your time listening rather than talking is difficult to learn at first. It is a skill that must be cultivated into a habit, but it will go a long way toward making you a good communicator.

PUT THE OTHER PERSON AT EASE

When either participant in a conversation is tense, it's very difficult for communication to take place. That's because rather than focusing on what you are discussing, he will be preoccupied with his own fears.

As you begin a conversation with someone, especially someone you don't know well or who you know is often tense or shy, try to discern her tension level. First, watch her eyes. The avoidance of eye contact, or a blank look, can indicate that a person is tense or shy. Certain types of body language can also indicate it: crossed arms, fidgeting, clenched teeth, an overly stiff posture, leaning away from the person speaking, etc. Finally, you might notice that people who are not at ease are often reluctant to talk. They tend to give very short answers to questions.

When you discover that someone you wish to talk with is tense or shy, it's important to put him or her at ease; otherwise, your ability to communicate will be limited. First, be friendly and smile. Nothing sets a person at ease more quickly. Second, be a good host. Give the person a comfortable place to sit. Offer something to drink or eat, if appropriate. Finally, start by talking about subjects that are fun and interesting to the other person. Ask about his family, hobbies, or background. As you establish rapport, the other person will probably relax and feel free to talk.

SHOW THAT YOU WANT TO LISTEN

An important aspect of positive communication is non-verbal feedback—gestures and body language. The non-verbal response a person gives can often determine the depth of the conversation. Negative feedback will restrict communication, while positive feedback enhances and encourages it.

One of the best ways to encourage communication is to show the other person that you want to listen to him. Look and act interested in his comments. Conveying this begins when you personally develop a genuine desire to be attentive. It's also important to focus on your understanding of what the person has to say rather than your response to it.

Negative feedback restricts communication. Positive feedback enhances and encourages it.

Just remember, any time your focus is wrong, you're more likely to misunderstand. You can't listen effectively if you're too busy formulating a response.

ASK QUESTIONS

When appropriate, ask questions to get additional information to clarify a point. Besides increasing your understanding, it will encourage the other person and show that you are listening. It also gives you additional time to process what you hear and still remain focused on them.

Focus on your understanding
*of what the person has to say, rather than
your* response *to it.*

As you ask questions, be sure to express them in an encouraging or neutral way. If the other person feels like you're doubting or challenging him, it will hinder rather than aid in communicating.

REMOVE DISTRACTIONS

Be sensitive to distractions that can hinder communication. Some people have a difficult time communicating over noise or music. Others have difficulties with physical distractions, such as an uncomfortable chair or bright sunlight in their faces. Try your best to remove distractions, and certainly avoid doodling, writing, tapping, and shuffling papers while talking with others. Not only is it distracting, but it communicates that the speaker's words have limited importance to you.

*Your goal is not only to understand the content
of the other person's message
but to assure him that you respect him
and what he has to say.*

BE PATIENT

Everyone communicates in his own unique way and at his own pace. It's important to respect that. Don't interrupt, even if you are pretty sure that you know what the other guy is about to say. Your goal is not only to understand the content of his message, but to assure him that you respect him and what he has to say. Your patience shows him that. Benjamin Disraeli said, "Patience is a necessary ingredient of genius." It is also a necessary ingredient of communication.

EMPATHIZE

One of the greatest aids to communication is empathy. If every person were compassionate toward his fellow man and tried his best to empathize instead of criticize, we would have fewer arguments and miscommunications.

---

*When we put ourselves
in the other person's place,
we're less likely to want to
"put him in his place."*

When speaking with another person, try your best to see things from his point of view. Try to understand why he thinks the way he does. As someone once said, when we put ourselves in the other person's place, we're less likely to want to "put him in his place."

DON'T TRY TO COMMUNICATE WHILE ANGRY

Everyone gets angry from time to time. It's a part of life. But when that anger comes while we're trying to communicate, the results can be disastrous. Anger often changes the meaning of words. And an angry person will often say things that he regrets later. It also blocks our ability to listen.

Avoid anger when trying to communicate. If you feel yourself getting angry during a conversation, try to hold your anger until later. If you can't, you may want to postpone the conversation until a time when you can speak more rationally. And whenever you're angry, don't choose that moment to seek out the object of your anger in order to try to resolve the issue. Wait until you have calmed down.

AVOID ARGUING AND CRITICIZING

Two of the most damaging practices to avoid in communication are arguing and criticizing. Neither one builds up the conversation; in fact, they both tend to tear it down.

Always do your best to build others up instead of tearing them down with criticism. And in situations where you must offer a contrary point of view or give correction, do it as positively as possible. Try to address the other person's actions without condemning him as a person. For example, you might tell him, "I know that you are a good worker and always try to do the right thing. We value your contribution to the team. That's the reason I want to help you correct something that happened yesterday. . . ." When you approach things from the most positive angle possible, you usually get positive results.

ALWAYS ANSWER A QUESTION DIRECTLY AND THEN EXPLAIN

A common characteristic of poor communicators is that they answer simple questions with complicated explanations. In contrast, most successful people focus on results. A process-oriented answer to a results-oriented question tends to make the questioner impatient, and it makes the responder appear evasive. Later, the questioner will probably repeat the question in search of a more direct response.

If you are in the habit of answering questions indirectly, remind yourself that most listeners prefer a more concise response. Then try to develop a more direct communication style. At the same time, be sure you don't go to the other extreme of answering with a simple yes or no answer. Give a little information—a little of the "why" behind your answer. It assures your listener that you know what you're talking about and aren't guessing. Just don't overload them with inconsequential details.

PRECEDE QUESTIONS WITH NECESSARY INFORMATION

Answers are best when they are direct, but questions often require a different approach. Most of us have probably been asked an unexpected and baffling question. We aren't sure what its subject is or why it's being asked. As a result, we have a hard time giving an answer.

Any time you ask a question, precede it with enough information to provide the context and intent of the question. You don't have to give a lot of information or tell a lengthy story. Just convey enough information so that the person can answer easily. For example, here are two ways to ask the same question:

1. "What does "PD" mean?"
2. "I'd like to ask you a question. I was reviewing the accounts last night, and I came across an abbreviation in the computer that I didn't understand. What does "PD" mean?

As you can see, a little information can really make a big difference in your question.

MAKE YOUR POINT EARLY

We live in a very busy world, where time is often the most precious commodity we have. As a result, communication is usually best when it's to the point. The less time and energy we have to spend working at communicating, the better it is for us. And anything we can do to avoid miscommunication is a bonus.

Whether you are communicating with people one-on-one or in a group, it's important that you make your point early—and then give additional explanation afterward. It not only saves everyone's time, but it also keeps your listener from having to guess at what you're leading up to. This prevents him from jumping to the wrong conclusion. Sometimes the explanation that you were prepared to give isn't even needed by the other person, because the point itself is clear enough without it.

BE CLEAR ABOUT THE SCOPE OF YOUR SUBJECT

A lot of misunderstanding can be avoided and wasted discussion prevented by making clear how big a problem is, how much work is going to be involved in a project, how much money an idea will cost, etc. Giving quantity or size to the subject alerts your listener to think along the same lines. Always communicate that small things are small and big things are big.

REPEAT YOURSELF TO GET YOUR POINT ACROSS

Professional speakers who communicate effectively understand the importance of repetition. Listeners often don't hear something the first time if they're still concentrating on what was said earlier. Repetition is also an excellent way to emphasize one point or subject over another.

Many people overlook the value of repetition in one-on-one conversation. But it can be an effective tool. Whenever you aren't sure if the other person understood you, try putting your message in other words or summarizing it.

TRY TO GET A RESPONSE FROM YOUR LISTENER

It's important to observe your listener's non-verbal feedback, but nothing is better at verifying the effectiveness of your communication than a verbal response from your listener. Give him a chance to respond, by encouraging him to put your message into his own words, or to ask questions at appropriate times. Make sure he understands an important point before moving on to the next one. Remember, if he remains silent, there is no way to know if your message has gotten across.

Nothing is better at verifying
the effectiveness of your communication
than a verbal response
from your listener.

ASK FOR YOUR LISTENER'S OPINION WHEN
YOU SENSE DISAGREEMENT

A common mistake of inexperienced communicators is to think that disagreement can be overcome by strengthening or lengthening their argument or point of view. But experienced communicators realize that more talking is not the answer. What's needed is more listening. In most cases, you can reach agreement if you give the other person a chance to talk and learn why she disagrees with you or objects to your idea. There are often factors that you weren't aware of. And often the objection is easy to address once you know what it is. Discussion is the way to get facts out in the open.

INCREASE YOUR CHANCES
FOR A FAVORABLE RESPONSE

Even when you have positive communication skills and use them effectively, you can still have difficulty communicating with people as effectively as you would like. This is especially true when you're presenting new or different ideas, since people tend to resist new ideas at first. Here are three possible normal responses:

Rejection: Often a new idea will meet with strong opposition at first. After you present it, the person says, "It won't work." And when you ask, "Why?" he replies, "Because we've tried it before and failed;" or "No one has ever done it before."

Tolerance: If the person responds to your idea by saying something like, "Well, I'll accept it as long as . . ." then you have received partial acceptance. As long as you meet or encourage them to modify their conditions, you can proceed.

Acceptance: If the person accepts your idea willingly and whole-heartedly, you can get started right away.

It's possible to increase your chances for a favorable response when presenting an idea. To do that, you must make sure the four conditions for that favorable response are met:

1. The person can and does understand the idea. Except in cases where they are compelled to comply, people will not accept an idea unless they understand it. If you are trying to get others to accept your idea, don't even try to gain their approval until you've communicated enough for them to fully comprehend it.

2. The person believes the idea is compatible with his own personal interests. When people are exposed to a new idea, one of the first questions they always ask (aloud or silently) is, "How is this going to affect me?" No one readily accepts anything that would cause more harm than good. So always remember to include information on the benefits of the idea when you present it. At the very least, show that it will not hurt your listeners.

3. The person believes the idea is not inconsistent with the purpose of the organization. While everyone asks how an idea will affect them personally, most also ask how it will affect the organization. They truly don't want their organization damaged. Dedicated people will insist on knowing that any new idea is an improvement. Therefore, be sure to outline the benefits of the new idea to the organization.

4. The person is mentally and physically able to comply with the idea. Even when you say all the right things, the people understand your idea, and they are convinced that it's

120

beneficial, they won't accept it if they aren't convinced that they can do it. Sometimes all you will have to provide is encouragement. Other times you'll have to anticipate problems and give explanations that prevent discouragement. You might also have to provide training or equipment to help your people.

DEVELOP SMALL GROUP COMMUNICATION SKILLS

The ability to communicate with small groups of people is becoming increasingly important nowadays, since leaders are spending more and more time facilitating group activities. In fact, American management expert Kenneth Blanchard has observed that managers in the United States spend from 60 to 90 percent of their time in group activities, yet they receive little to no training in that area.

Small group communication builds on one-on-one communication, but with different dynamics. It has been said that a small group meeting is a place where everybody talks, nobody listens, and everyone discusses afterward. And it really is peculiar—some people won't communicate much in front of others even when they are a recognized authority on the subject, while others will say things in the safety of a group that they would never say one-on-one.

Because these dynamics can complicate communication, a specific small-group strategy is necessary. Here's a three-part formula for success in small groups.

1. KNOW YOUR PEOPLE

Each person in your group has a different personality and unique strengths and weaknesses. Recognize that they are different and cannot be treated the same. It's also important to discover the key to each person's personality, then use it. Here are eleven common personalities that can emerge in a group setting, and some tips on how to best deal with them:

The Eager Beaver. An Eager Beaver is the quick, helpful type—the first to jump in with an opinion. But in spite of good intentions, this person can make things difficult when his chatter prevents others from contributing. Affirm the Eager

Beaver's helpful nature by asking him to summarize what was discussed at the end of the meeting. And when necessary, tactfully divert attention from him by asking questions of others. Or thank him for his input and suggest that "we put others to work." If you can tactfully keep him from monopolizing the conversation, the Eager Beaver can be a positive contributor to the team, especially when it's time to summarize what has been said.

The Immovable Object. The Immovable Object is a naturally stubborn or obstinate person who tends to resist all ideas and suggestions. When riled, she looks like she couldn't be budged with a bulldozer. The best way to handle her negative input is to ask the group to comment on it. This way, you leave it to them to point out when she's out of line. Then if the Immovable Object continues offering negative opinions, state that you'll be glad to discuss her views *after the meeting*, but that she needs to accept the group viewpoint for the time being.

The Dampener. The Dampener always feels compelled to point out the worst aspects of every idea suggested. But seldom—if ever—does he volunteer a better alternative. The best way to handle him is to insist that he suggest an alternative every time he points out something negative. Then indicate that you understand his objections and restate the good points of his suggested solution. In addition, ask other members of the group to comment on his remarks.

The Indiscriminate Agreer. The Indiscriminate Agreer is an amiable person who will agree wholeheartedly with any suggestion, no matter how good or bad it is. Because of her eagerness to agree, you can't put much faith in her stated opinions. Acknowledge their remarks politely, and then ask for the opinions of more discerning members of the group.

The Indiscriminate Arguer. An Indiscriminate Arguer is a combative person who either enjoys being contrary or is upset by personal problems. Alarmingly, if you have two in one group, and they clash, they're capable of dividing the group into factions. The best way to deal with the Indiscriminate Arguer is to focus on the objective of the meeting. If he starts to argue, emphasize the points on which you can agree. Cut across the argument with a direct question on the original topic of the discussion. If necessary, ask frankly that personalities be omitted from the meeting.

The Inarticulate Talker. The Inarticulate Talker is someone who has good ideas but has great difficulty in expressing her thoughts. The best way to handle her is to repeat her ideas in better language—without hurting her feelings. Don't use phrases like "What you mean is . . ." or "This is what you are trying to say. . ." Instead, say something like, "What a great idea! Bob, what do you think of Sue's suggestion to . . .?" And then restate it more clearly. Don't modify her ideas any more than you have to in order to make sense.

The Side Conversationalist. The Side Conversationalist continuously talks privately to others during the meeting. Whether the conversation is related to the subject of the meeting or not, it distracts group members, especially the speaker. When handling the Side Conversationalist, try to avoid embarrassing him. Instead, call him by name and ask him an easy question. Or restate the last remark made by a group member and have the Side Conversationalist express his opinion of it. This communicates that his participation in the discussion is important and will often serve to bring him back into the group.

The Rambler. The Rambler seems to enjoy expressing her opinion on every subject except the one being discussed. She may start on the current subject, but she won't stay there long. After a few of her far-fetched analogies or comments, the entire group can get hopelessly lost. The best way to handle the Rambler is to refocus her attention on the subject at hand as soon as she stops to take a breath. Get her back on the track by restating relevant points, then move on. It also works to state that her point is interesting and then, with a smile, point out that, "we're a bit off the subject." As a last resort, glance meaningfully at your watch.

The Silent One. There can be a variety of reasons for the Silent One's refusal to talk: timidity, insecurity, superiority, indifference, or boredom. Whatever his reasons, he won't be an asset to the group unless you draw him out. The action you take will depend upon what is motivating him. Try to arouse his interest by asking him a question. If he's seated near you, ask his opinion—he might speak up if he feels he is talking to you, not the group. Toss out a provocative query to see if it will stir him. If you discover that he's shy, sometimes a sincere compliment for his comment is enough to draw him out.

The Inattentive One. The Inattentive One seems to be present in body but not in mind. To get her interested, try to gain her attention inconspicuously. Ask the Inattentive One a specific question that you know she can answer. Or restate an opinion that was shared and ask what she thinks of it. Sometimes it helps to preface a question with, "Would everyone think carefully about this next question and form his own answer?"

The Griper. Whether giving loud voice to a pet peeve or a legitimate complaint, the Griper wastes precious time and dampens the spirit of any meeting. To deal with him, remind him of time constraints. If he brings up a private matter, tell him you'll be happy to discuss it later. If he complains about something that isn't easily changed, point that out and encourage him to make the effort to operate as smoothly as possible under the present system. An alternative is to have a positive member of the group answer his complaints.

When you learn to deal positively with problem people, it becomes easier to work with everyone in the group. And then you can really get a lot accomplished.

2. SHOW YOUR PEOPLE

Nothing can frustrate and irritate a group of motivated people faster than a leader who isn't prepared for a meeting. It's crucial not only to be prepared, but to demonstrate that you know what you're doing—and that following you is their best course of action.

When preparing for a meeting, use these six steps:

1. Prepare an agenda. This not only shows your people that you are prepared and know where you want to go, but also enables them to join you in the journey. Create your agenda ahead of time, making sure it's very clear and straightforward. Then you have the option of distributing it to the group ahead of time so they'll have no surprises. The agenda should include information items (which will not require action), study items (which are to be discussed but

not voted on in this meeting), and action items (which were previously study items and are now ready for action through voting).

2. Meet with key group members individually before the meeting and prepare them through discussion. If you meet with key individuals ahead of time, they get a chance to examine and think through key issues before they come up in the meeting. This way, you have their support when you need it, and they aren't put on the spot.

3. Use visual aids when possible. Most people are visual learners. Use graphs, illustrations, and pictures to give life to projections and planning.

4. Predict possible questions and have the answers ready before the meeting. Do your best to avoid getting "sideswiped." When you've thought through potential objections, you'll do a better job presenting ideas, and members will know you're prepared.

5. Enter the meeting with confidence, sincerity, positiveness, and openness. Most of the people in the group will follow your lead in terms of attitude, so it's important to demonstrate the traits that you want them to emulate.

6. Understand and avoid common hindrances to effective meetings. Executives have identified a number of reasons why meetings can fall flat. Here are several:

   a. Meetings are held on a regular basis, even when there is nothing to be discussed.
   b. Participants neglect to do their homework, and the result is digression and disorganization.
   c. The person in charge doesn't know how to conduct a meeting.
   d. The meeting is held in an atmosphere which is not conducive to good discussion.
   e. The meeting lasts too long.

Anticipating and avoiding these common problems can greatly improve your ability to accomplish things when you meet with your people.

3. GROW YOUR PEOPLE

As a leader, you have the privilege of helping your people move from where they are now to where they need to be. Take responsibility for this and develop them. This can be accomplished in the following ways.

1. Teach them. Spend time on a regular basis—in meetings and one-on-one—teaching your group members. Give them training in areas of weakness. Make them better at their jobs—with their own personal benefit in mind.

2. Expose them to other good leaders. There are many good leaders and thinkers who can help your people develop new skills. Suggest articles, books, and tapes that will help them grow and learn. Arrange for them to spend time with people you respect who can teach them.

3. Enlarge and empower them by delegating responsibilities to each member. Don't delegate responsibilities only to get a particular job done. It's also important to keep in mind each person's development. Sometimes you can help a person expand his horizons or increase his abilities through delegation—by empowering him to tackle a new area of responsibility. This ends up being a win-win situation for everyone.

Learning to communicate effectively is a process that takes time. If you don't have much experience, you may find it difficult at first. Expect to make some mistakes. But as you practice, you'll improve.

When you do begin to communicate more effectively, a whole new world will present itself. You will be able to go places and do things that you once thought were impossible. And you will be better in a position to motivate and lead others to go with you.

SUCCESS STRATEGY ACTIVITIES

1. The next time you are in a restaurant, park, or other public place where you can watch people, observe any pairs who are engaged in conversation. Make note of their facial expressions,

body language and hand gestures, and try to determine their meaning. Develop a body language "vocabulary" that you can recognize. Then use that knowledge to communicate better in the future.

2.   Complete the following questionnaire to determine your communication strengths and weaknesses. Then have someone you know well, like your spouse or a close friend, complete it again for you so you'll know how others perceive your communication skills.

COMMUNICATION QUESTIONNAIRE

SCALE
1 = Never   2 = Rarely   3 = Sometimes   4 = Usually   5 = Always

1. In conversations, I speak less than 50 percent of the time.   1-2-3-4-5

2. I know almost immediately whether the person I am talking with is comfortable or tense.   1-2-3-4-5

3. I consciously do things to put others at ease in conversation.   1-2-3-4-5

4. I make an effort to ask simple questions to demonstrate that I am listening and interested.   1-2-3-4-5

5. I consciously remove distractions when speaking with others.   1-2-3-4-5

6. I am patient and do not interrupt others as they are speaking.   1-2-3-4-5

7. I really make an effort to really see the other person's point of view when mine is different.   1-2-3-4-5

8. I don't start–or allow myself to be drawn into–arguments.   1-2-3-4-5

9. I don't criticize others, even when I need to correct them.   1-2-3-4-5

10. When someone asks a question, I give a short, direct answer and avoid giving unsolicited explanations.   1-2-3-4-5

11. I do not ask abrupt questions that people find difficult to answer.   1-2-3-4-5

12. When I talk to others, I try to make my point within the first 30 seconds.   1-2-3-4-5

13. I repeat, rephrase, and summarize what I'm trying   1-2-3-4-5
to communicate when my listener doesn't appear
to understand.

14. I regularly ask for a response from my listener to be   1-2-3-4-5
sure he understands what I am trying to say.

15. When I sense that the other person disagrees, I stop   1-2-3-4-5
talking, ask for his opinion, and let him give his
point of view before I address his objections.

KEY

60 - 75	You have excellent communication skills
45 - 59	You have good communication skills
35 - 44	Your communication skills are average
Below 35	Your communication skills are below average

By totaling your score, along with the score the other person gave you, you can get a general idea of your level of skill. Review the questionnaire to find your weakest areas, reread the sections that deal with those areas, and then use them to begin improving those skills. Complete the questionnaire again in three months to determine your progress.

3.   The next time you plan to present a new idea, mentally determine whether the four required conditions have been met before you ask for a response:

    a.   The person can and does understand the idea.

    b.   The person believes the idea is compatible with his own personal interests.

    c.   The person believes the idea is not inconsistent with the purpose of the organization.

    d.   The person is able mentally and physically to comply with the idea.

4.   Set aside some time to analyze the people in any group you regularly lead. Write their names down on a 3 X 5 card, and then identify which type of person each is according to the list given in the

chapter. Write down next to the name one or two words which will remind you of the strategy to use with each of them in your next meeting. Review the card several times a day for a week prior to the meeting.

5. Plan your next meeting according to the guidelines in the chapter. Prepare your agenda; meet with key people ahead of time; prepare visual aids; prepare for any questions that the people may have; and begin the meeting positively and openly. Also be sensitive to avoid the common hindrances to effective meetings.

———————

-chapter nine-

The Successful Person Believes in ...
MOTIVATION

Motivation is the art of getting people to do what you want them to do because they want to do it.

—Dwight D. Eisenhower

No man will make a great leader who wants to do it all himself, or to get all the credit for doing it.

—Andrew Carnegie

It's been said that three things move the world, and the first two are: coming up with ideas and getting people to like them. So far, you've received quite a bit of information about coming up with ideas and communicating with people. But what about putting the two together—getting people to like your ideas? That's where the ability to motivate people becomes important.

THE MEANING OF MOTIVATION
What does it mean to motivate someone else? *Webster's New World Dictionary of the English Language* says that the word motivate means "to provide with ... a motive." And motive means "some inner drive ... that causes a person to ... act in a certain way." So motivation can be defined as connecting with something inside of a person which causes him to act.

Some people tend to hope that an outside force will move them and those around them in the direction they need to go. But any time the force that moves us comes from outside of us, the movement is temporary. It's like the difference between a car with gasoline and one without. When a car is out of gas, it has to be pushed. And as soon as we stop pushing, it immediately loses momentum and comes to a stop. But a full gas tank in that same car fuels the motor within. And it keeps moving almost indefinitely.

Motivation is the internal fuel for us. Without motivation, it's hard to get going—and impossible to build up momentum. And once outside forces are removed, we tend to come to a stop. But when we're empowered by ongoing motivation, we're on our way to continued success.

> *Motivation is connecting*
> *with something inside of a person*
> *which causes him to act.*

To help others move forward—and accept your ideas—you must learn to motivate them, and do it from within. You must put "gas in their gas tanks."

In a recent poll, seventy psychologists were asked to identify the most critical thing that a supervisor must know about human nature. Over 65 percent of them said it was motivation, an understanding of what makes people feel and act as they do. If you don't understand motivation, you can't motivate others. Without motivation, you cannot lead others. And if you cannot lead others, you will have to achieve everything you wish to accomplish on your own. How limiting!

MOTIVATION BEGINS WITH YOU

How does a person get started motivating others? By first motivating himself. It's impossible to motivate someone else when you are not motivated, because people are not convinced by someone who doesn't "walk his talk." No one follows a person who is not first committed to going himself.

> *It's impossible to motivate someone else*
> *when you are not motivated.*

One of my favorite figures from history is King David of Israel (ca. 1000 B.C.). He was an excellent example of a man whose inner motivation inspired and motivated others. When David was a young man and not yet king, he once delivered food to his brothers in the army. While near the battle lines, he saw a giant named Goliath, the champion from the opposing army. The giant was mocking the soldiers in Israel's army, and he struck fear into all of their hearts, including the heart of their king, Saul. But not in David. He was motivated to challenge and fight Goliath. And David killed him.

Before David, there were no giant-killers in Saul's army. But after David the giant-killer became King, many giant-killers arose in his army.

Why do you suppose there were no giant-killers in King Saul's army? Saul himself was not a giant-killer. He was not willing to face the giant as a warrior for his people. However, through David's example, many soldiers also became motivated to be giant-killers.

If you are having trouble motivating yourself, here are several suggestions to help you get going:

1. Add up the rewards of beginning and the cost of neglecting to start. Sometimes when we have trouble getting started, we need to remind ourselves of the good things that will happen if we begin. Or we might need to list the negative things that will happen if we don't start. It's just like starting a diet. It's easier to get motivated if we keep in mind that we will look better and feel healthier if we lose weight. Or we can think about the negative effects on our health if we don't get started.

Breaking down a larger project
into smaller, doable tasks
makes the whole thing seem achievable,
and that's motivating.

---

2. Generate a sense of urgency. The next hurdle you face after convincing yourself that you should begin is getting yourself actually to start. It sometimes helps to create a sense of urgency. Instead of choosing the last possible moment to get started, use the opposite perspective. Ask yourself, "When is the earliest I can do this?" It can also help to make your goals public for added incentive.

3. Make out a schedule now. Another way to get going is to plan your actions according to a schedule. Seeing them written down often provides incentive. Plus, breaking down a larger project into smaller, doable tasks makes the whole thing seem achievable, and that's motivating.

4. Don't wait until you feel like it to get started. This is one of the most common mistakes we make in motivation. Don't fall into this trap. It's a rare person who actually feels like getting started before he's involved. It's more effective to start now because you know it's the right thing to do. Your feelings will tend to follow your actions.

5. Don't wait until you see solutions to every problem before you get started. Samuel Johnson said, "Nothing will be attempted if all possible obstacles must first be removed." High achievers spot rich opportunities swiftly, make big decisions quickly, and then move into action immediately. Do your best to solve the crucial problems, but don't let perfectionism paralyze you. Go ahead and get started when you've done what you can.

Personal motivation gets things started, because it leads to action. And it also creates momentum, which is invaluable to achievement. For example, have you ever thought about how little it takes to keep a motionless locomotive from getting started? If you were to put a single one-inch block of wood in front of each of its drive wheels, that train would not be able to move. But if that same locomotive were already moving at 60 miles per hour, it would have the power and momentum to crash through a wall of steel-reinforced concrete that's five feet thick!

The same is true for a person with motivated momentum. Once he's moving forward, he can overcome incredible obstacles.

PRINCIPLES FOR MOTIVATING OTHER PEOPLE

Motivating yourself to get going and gain momentum is one thing, but inspiring others is another matter. While your own motivation does serve as a model for others, you also need to develop strategies that can further influence their actions. Use the following ideas to give people around you an extra boost of motivation:

COMMUNICATE WITH CLARITY

Lawyers admit today that over half of all the controversies that arise among people are caused not by differences of opinion or even inability to agree, but rather by lack of understanding. If this is true, think how much confusion and misinformation is possible in our daily lives if we're not able to make ourselves understood.

> *Motivation must always begin with*
> *clarity of communication.*

When trying to motivate others, we cannot afford misunderstandings. Motivation must always begin with clarity of communication. After all, people can't do what they don't understand. So always be sure you know exactly what you're asking of others before you start talking. Do your very best to communicate it as simply and clearly as you can, and let your listeners ask questions and clarify whatever they don't understand.

BE COMMITTED TO A PURPOSE

The most persuasive person in the world is someone with complete confidence in his idea, product, or service. Likewise, the common denominator of all great men in history is that they believed in what they were doing. They were dedicated and committed to their purpose, and others were eager to follow them.

The CEO of a large corporation was once asked how he selected people for difficult assignments. He said that he always looked for someone who was convinced that the job could be done and would be dedicated to completing it. The executive knew that confidence like that would motivate the employee to complete the assignment and also inspire those around him.

> *People are more persuaded by the*
> *depth of our convictions than by the*
> *height of our logic.*

What it comes down to is that people are more persuaded by the depth of our convictions than by the height of our logic. They respond more to our own enthusiasm than to any proof we can offer. If you desire to motivate others, show them your commitment.

GIVE PEOPLE RECOGNITION

Few things motivate us better than praise. We tend to respond in proportion to others' expectations of us. So when I say that my people are doing a great job, it makes them want to work even harder to continue meeting my expectations.

> *We tend to respond in proportion to others' expectations of us.*

Praise is always useful, but when it is given publicly, its benefits multiply. Not only does the person being praised work harder, but he also gains a positive reputation. This enhances his value to others and motivates them to be like him.

I once heard a story that shows how effective this is. A few months after moving to a small town, a woman complained to her neighbor about the poor service she had received at the local drugstore. She knew that her neighbor was a friend of the owner and hoped the neighbor would repeat her complaint to him.

The next time she went to the drugstore, the druggist greeted her with a big smile and told her how happy he was to see her again. He said he hoped she liked their town, and expressed his willingness to help her and her husband get settled in. He then filled her order promptly and efficiently.

Elated with this change, the woman reported the miraculous change to her neighbor. "I suppose you told the druggist how poor I thought the service was?" she asked.

"Well no," the neighbor said. "In fact—and I hope you don't mind—I told him you were amazed at the way he had built up this small-town business and that you thought it was one of the best-run drugstores you had ever seen."

CREATE FRIENDLY COMPETITION

People have a naturally competitive spirit, and connecting with that spirit can create positive motivation. In his book, *How to Win*

Friends and Influence People, Dale Carnegie tells the story of a mill manager who worked under the leadership of Charles Schwab, a master motivator. The men weren't producing their quota of work, and Schwab asked the manager how someone as capable as he couldn't make the mill produce as it should.

"I don't know," the man replied, "I've coaxed the men, I've pushed them; I've sworn and cussed; I've threatened them with damnation and being fired, but nothing works. They just won't produce."

This conversation happened to be occurring at the end of the day, just before the night shift began. Schwab suddenly asked the manager to give him a piece of chalk. Then he turned to a worker and asked, "How many heats did your shift make today?"

"Six," answered the worker.

Then Schwab simply wrote a big "6" on the floor and walked away.

When the night shift came in soon after that, they saw the "6" and asked what it meant. Of course, they were told that the big boss had visited the mill, asked how many heats the day shift had produced, and chalked the number on the floor.

The next morning, Schwab walked through the mill again. But this time he saw that the night shift had rubbed out the "6" on the floor and replaced it with a "7." When the day shift reported for work, they saw that big "7" and were inspired by a sense of competition. So they decided to show the night shift a thing or two and pitched in with enthusiasm. When the day shift finished working, they left behind them a remarkable "10."

Soon the mill, which had been way behind in production, was turning out more work than any other mill in the plant. Schwab's comment: "The way to get things done is to stimulate competition. I do not mean in a sordid, money-getting way, but in the desire to excel."

GIVE THEM A LITTLE AT A TIME

Have you noticed that when you learn a new task, you often reach a point of "overload," when your brain can no longer absorb any new information? That's a normal human reaction. We all learn better bit-by-bit. So if you're training or attempting to motivate others, it's not good to give them too much information too soon.

136

As you've probably experienced personally, receiving too much input can actually demotivate a person. When he's unable to use or apply all the information he receives, he'll tend to forget much of it. Confusion can set in, and he'll probably be too embarrassed to ask questions. The whole experience becomes negative, and he learns to avoid situations like that in the future.

To avoid a negative experience, give those you're trying to motivate only enough information to whet their appetites. This will create a desire to try out the new information, and the opportunity to apply it. Every time they apply what they learn, they're better able to remember it. And they also achieve small successes, which motivate them to learn more.

STRENGTHEN PERSONAL RELATIONSHIPS

Have you ever noticed how easy it is to respond positively to the people who matter most to you? The needs and desire of friends and loved ones are probably more important to you than those of strangers. You tend to be willing to follow someone you like. And when you care about someone, it's much easier to become motivated by them.

If you desire to motivate people around you, nothing yields a higher return than strengthening your relationships with them. As a rule, let those you want to lead get to know you better; likewise, take time to learn more about them. As you discover common interests, you'll establish common bonds, making it easier to motivate and direct them.

LET PEOPLE EXPERIENCE RESULTS AND REWARDS

A psychology professor once conducted an experiment to see how much results mattered to people. He hired a lumberjack to hit a log all day—but with the blunt side of the ax. The man was told that he would work his normal hours, but would be paid twice the amount he normally made. His only task was to hit that log with the ax. The lumberjack began the task eagerly enough, but he quit after only half a day. When asked why, he replied, "I have to see the chips fly."

The people around us are like that lumberjack. They receive personal fulfillment when they see results. It's what keeps many of them going. The auto worker likes to see the finished car ready to drive down the road. The chef doing the catering wants to know that his work has made the banquet a success. The riveter who works on the space shuttle gets tremendous satisfaction from watching it launch into space.

If you want to motivate people—especially those whose work is only a part of something greater—reward them with results. Show them the finished product. Let them know how their contribution fits into the bigger picture. When they know they are making a difference, they'll be encouraged—and willing to continue the work.

How we see a person determines the level at which he functions for us.

BELIEVE IN THEM

All people want to matter to others, to know that they're important. One way to motivate your people is to let them know that you believe in them. Express your confidence in their potential to become the persons they would like to become. Give them hope and reveal a glimpse of the bright future that is possible for them.

How we see a person determines the level at which he functions for us. If we see him as a problem, that is what he will become. If we see him as a success, he will be a success.

APPROACHES TO MOTIVATION

The previous eight ideas are foundational. They are basic skills without which you will have a difficult time motivating others. But without this final skill, you can't become a master motivator, because not all people can be motivated in the same way.

Frank O. Prior, chairman of the Standard Oil Company, recognized that no single technique can be used for motivating everyone. He said, "Some men you smile at, some you counsel, some you swear at. You work with them under policies and principles as individuals, or they silently rebel."

No matter which approach you use in motivating people, I recommend one that I value above all others: example. People follow your footsteps more quickly than your advice. As Albert Schweitzer said, "Example is not the main thing in influencing others. It is the only thing."

> *People follow your footsteps*
> *more quickly than your advice.*

George Washington, the commanding general during the American Revolution and the first President of the United States, was a motivator who led by example. One day during the Revolutionary War, General Washington rode up to a group of soldiers trying to raise a heavy beam to a high position. The corporal stood at a distance, shouting words of encouragement, but to no avail. Washington observed for a few moments, then asked why he did not join in and help.

The corporal replied quickly, "Don't you realize that I am the corporal?"

Washington very politely replied, "I beg your pardon, Mr. Corporal. I did not realize it."

General Washington then dismounted his horse and joined the soldiers in their labor until the beam was put into place. When the job was finished, he wiped the perspiration from his face and told the amazed group of enlisted men, "If you should need help again, call on Washington, your commander-in-chief, and I will come."

> *A leader's example offers an unspoken,*
> *yet powerful, motivator.*

A leader's example offers an unspoken, yet powerful, motivator. But sometimes something more is necessary—an appeal for commitment. Here are seven types of appeals that you can use to motivate others. They offer a variety of approaches that appeal to just about everyone:

1. APPEAL TO BENEFITS

This is one of the most common appeals used in the business of sales. The benefits mentioned can directly affect either the person being motivated or others. And they can be nearly anything: emotional, financial, intellectual, physical, etc. You can motivate someone to exercise by describing the physical benefits. You can persuade someone to invest his money in order to reap financial rewards during retirement. You can convince someone to buy clothes because they will make him feel good about himself.

Here's one important reminder. Never try to motivate someone else by explaining the benefits that you will receive from their compliance. Nothing will turn them off faster. Most people don't mind if you both benefit from your partnership. But for the most part, they really want to know, "What's in it for me?" Make sure to focus on the benefits those you lead will receive, and you'll avoid offending or manipulating them.

2. APPEAL TO EMOTIONS

Emotional appeals can be very powerful. In fact, most of the great orators throughout history have used them with great success. As an historian said of Napoleon Bonaparte, "Half of what he achieved was achieved by the power of words."

An emotional appeal can move people to act quickly and with fervor. Humor, love, hate, fear, compassion, and anger all have a galvanizing effect. But beware: Emotions do move people, but they can also be fleeting. Motivation based entirely on emotion can disappear as quickly as it appeared.

3. APPEAL TO NEEDS

This appeal is the most basic of all motivators, because everyone has needs. In fact, most of what we do every day is motivated by a desire to have needs met. As Douglas McGregor said, "Man is a wanting animal—as soon as one of his needs is satisfied, another appears in its place. This process is unending. It continues from birth to death. Man continuously puts forth effort—works, if you please—to satisfy his needs."

Appeals to needs can be directed to five areas:

1. The Need for Security: Security is the most basic of all needs, starting with the necessities of life, such as food, shelter, and clothing. But people also need and crave emotional security.
2. The Need for Love: The need for love affects a person throughout his life. Our lives are radically impacted by the

amount of love we received, or didn't receive, as children. Romantic love affects us in our youth and married years. And as we grow old, our need for love remains strong, as we strive to establish and sustain connections with our children, grandchildren, friends and other family. The desire for love is one of the strongest and longest-lasting motivators for all people.

3. The Need for Creative Expression: The need for creative expression can be found in all of us, even if it's faint. For some, such as the great artists and composers in history, this need is the driving force in their lives. Fulfilling it gives them the deepest satisfaction and greatest joy.

4. The Need for Recognition: No one wants to be a mere statistic. We all have a need to feel needed and important. For that reason, recognition can be the most dynamic of all motivating factors.

    A man named J.C. Staehle discovered this when he conducted a survey of workers. Asking about the causes of unrest among them, he noticed something interesting about the top five. They were: (1) failure to give credit for suggestions; (2) failure to correct grievances; (3) failure to encourage; (4) criticizing employees in front of other people; and (5) failure to ask employees their opinions. Staehle notice that all five had to do with a failure to recognize the employees' importance. Failure to give credit for work communicates, "Your work isn't very important." Failure to correct grievances says, "Your opinions and feelings are so unimportant that we can't be bothered with them."

When we speak to people's needs, we tap into something universal, into qualities we all share.

5. The Need for New Experiences: We all have an inherent need to experience new things. This need has motivated people to climb Mt. Everest, explore the wilds of Africa, and create new inventions. No one desires to stay exactly

141

where he is right now. We are always searching for something new, something better.

When we speak to people's needs, we tap into something universal, into qualities we all share. Needs have motivated some of the most noble and sublime achievements in our history.

4. APPEAL TO ABILITIES

Everyone loves being an authority on something. When you appeal to a person based on his abilities, you strengthen his sense of self-worth. You're communicating, "I want you to do this because you're the best at it. You are the expert." Charles Schwab understood this motivator, and used it effectively. "I have yet to find the man, however exalted his station, who did not do better work and put forth greater effort," he said, "under a spirit of approval than under a spirit of criticism." When you appeal to a person's abilities, it is the strongest way to express a spirit of approval.

5. APPEAL TO THE OCCASION

Sometimes circumstances give us great opportunities to motivate others. Recently the professional football team from our city went to the Super Bowl. It was quite an occasion because in its history, our team had never gone to that game before.

The people in the city went wild! The team and its success was the topic of hundreds of television and radio programs. It seemed like every conversation in the city was about the players and coaches. And the team's colors and logo were everywhere—on the sides of buildings downtown, on people's houses, in restaurants.

The team had people excited. And they were motivated—to buy souvenirs from the team, to plan parties, to talk to strangers when they normally didn't. It moved people to take action.

An occasion like that often gives you a chance to motivate others in a way you couldn't before. Sometimes the appeal doesn't have to relate directly to the event itself; it can simply use the momentum from the event to create excitement.

6. APPEAL TO LOYALTY

Most people are loyal to someone or something—their family, company, country, community, etc. That kind of loyalty creates a natural opportunity to motivate them, because they'll want to assist, improve, or defend whoever or whatever they are loyal to. And the greater the loyalty, the greater the potential for motivation. Just show them how the actions you propose will benefit the object of their loyalty.

7. APPEAL TO CONVICTIONS

The most lasting appeals are those that speak to people's lasting values—their convictions. Convictions are what we use to determine what is "right" or "wrong." And when we believe that we must commit or act because it is the right thing to do, it's easy to become, and remain, motivated.

> *The most lasting appeals*
> *are those that speak to*
> *people's lasting values—*
> *their convictions.*

Convictions vary not only from person to person but from one society to another. To motivate another person based on his convictions, we must consider his nationality, community, religious beliefs, class or socio-economic group, upbringing, family background, and culture. It's obviously easiest to motivate someone who shares your convictions, since less learning is required. But you can appeal to the convictions of another culture, as long as you take the time to discover and communicate them effectively.

All successful people must possess personal motivation. It gives them the will to persevere and overcome obstacles of all kinds. But successful leaders have another ability. They understand people and know how to motivate them. So they're able to accomplish a vision that is larger than themselves, by making use of the contribution of others.

Psychologists at the University of Michigan Research Center in Ann Arbor, Michigan, began a scientific study in 1949 which continues to this day. The researchers wanted to discover what makes people work harder, produce more and do better work. Through their studies, they have found that the foreman who expresses interest in his people gets more work from them than the bossy type who simply tries to force them to work harder.

Science Newsletter, in reporting on the findings of these scientists, said, "Pressuring for production may work to some degree. But the best results are achieved when a worker's internal motivations are tapped—his self-expression, self-determination, and sense of personal worth. A person works better when he is treated as a personality, given some degree of freedom in the way he does his work, and allowed to make his own decisions."

The ability to tap people's internal motivation can change the world.

The ability to tap people's internal motivation can change the world. When done with the right motives, it can create a win-win situation. It gives the people being motivated a reason to do what they really desire. And it helps the motivator to extend himself and his ability to achieve. This brings enlarged success to everyone.

SUCCESS STRATEGY ACTIVITIES

---

1. Pick an area of your life where you need to become motivated. It should be something that you believe you should do but have a hard time disciplining yourself to do. Then go through the process described in the chapter to get motivated:

   a. Add up the rewards of beginning and the cost of neglecting to begin. Write these down so that you can see them and make them concrete.

   b. Generate a sense of urgency. Determine the earliest date that you can get started, put it on your calendar, and then tell someone close to you what you intend to do. Ask that person to question you a few days after your start date to make sure you have followed through.

   c. Make out a schedule now. Break down your project into steps or smaller tasks. Then enter each task or activity on your calendar. And when possible, determine a target date for completion.

  d. Don't wait until you feel like it to get started. Start on your start date, and remind yourself that how you feel has nothing to do with beginning. Getting started on that first day is usually when you will feel the worst. Be prepared to persevere anyway, because it will get easier.

  e. Don't wait until you see solutions to every problem before you get started. Don't allow yourself to use problems as an excuse. Solve them as they come, and give yourself enough slack to make some mistakes along the way.

2. For one week, give others positive recognition as often as you can. Give team members credit for the successes of the team. Find something positive in everything that people do, and be sure to tell others about it. Praise people publicly, especially in front of their family and friends.

3. The next time you find yourself in a teaching or training situation, use the technique of giving a little information at a time. Provide a quick overview of the task so that the learner will know what direction he'll be going, and then give only enough additional information to get him started. Help him to immediately apply what he's learned so that he achieves some quick successes. Then give enough information for the next step, and once again help him apply it. Keep repeating the process until the task is learned.

4. Select one person whom you would like to be able to motivate more effectively than you currently do. It could be a co-worker, employee, acquaintance, or family member. Then work on building a closer relationship with that person. Attend a social function together. Have her over for dinner. Do a fun activity together that she likes. Sit down together and talk. In other words, get to know that person better and develop a positive relationship.

5. The next time you desire to motivate someone, before you begin, think about what is important to that other person—his needs and wants. Then form an appeal that speaks to those needs. Then use the appeal to persuade and motivate him or her.

145

-chapter ten-

The Successful Person Demonstrates . . .
LEADERSHIP

Leadership is not wielding authority — it's empowering people.
—Becky Brodin

The size of a leader is determined by the depth of his convictions, the height of his ambitions, the breadth of his vision, and the reach of his love.
—D.N. Jackson

Small victories can be achieved alone; but great victories, the kinds that ultimately bring success, can't be won by one person. To accomplish them, you must include other people. And any time you start involving others to achieve any goal, you cross over into the area of leadership. My friend John Maxwell has often said, "Everything rises and falls on leadership." And I believe he's right. When you know how to lead others effectively, you increase your potential and the potential of others to accomplish great things and fulfill your vision.

Everything rises and falls on leadership.

THE NATURE OF LEADERSHIP
What exactly is leadership? According to Warren G. Bennis, "Leadership is the capacity to translate vision into reality." In the broadest sense, that is true. But it's not a complete picture, since it only tells "what" leadership does. The all-important "how" of leader-

ship must include another element—other people. The method by which a leader makes his vision become a reality is through utilizing the efforts of others.

You might have heard it said that anyone who thinks he is a leader but has no one following him is merely taking a walk. So how does the person learning to lead actually encourage others to follow? Our culture tends to promote one common answer: that leadership gets its power from a position or title. Many believe that the boss is able to lead because he has the position, and the manager because he has the title. But that's a misconception; it's not the true nature of leadership. A person who can do no more than lead within the narrow parameters of his position is not a true leader. As John White said, "People do not follow programs, but leaders who inspire them."

> *Leadership begins with*
> *a person's character and vision—*
> *the core of who he is*
> *as a person.*

The best definition for leadership that I have seen is this: Leadership is influence. A true leader is able to influence others to follow him. He somehow gets them to join up and move out with him. The people around him choose to be willing extensions of his vision, goals, and accomplishments. Empowered to succeed, they eagerly participate in the leader's plan.

Leadership begins with a person's character and vision—the core of who he is as a person. As leadership expert Fred Smith said, "Leaders get out in front and stay there by raising the standards by which they judge themselves — and by which they are willing to be judged." The best leaders are continually growing, stretching, and learning. They are willing to pay the price of leadership—making the sacrifices necessary to continue improving themselves, enlarging their vision, increasing their skills, and reaching their potential. Through their example, they become people that others admire.

147

LEADERSHIP STYLES

In many ways, leadership starts within the leader, with his own determination and vision. It continues when the leader is able to assess where the people are and move them in the direction they need to go. Rosalyn Carter, wife of former U.S. President Jimmy Carter, said, "A leader takes people where they want to go. A great leader takes people where they don't necessarily want to go, but ought to be."

All leaders influence people, but each one does so differently, according to a variety of factors, including the personality, organization, culture and tradition of the people, and the timing and nature of a given issue. Although the foundational principles of leadership don't change, styles of leadership do. Thus, there is really no one right way to lead. Great leaders often adapt their leadership style based on whom they are leading. Here are five common leadership styles:

1. THE DOMINATING LEADER

The dominating leader focuses his attention on getting things accomplished, and he makes that happen by giving orders. He is not usually concerned with followers' reactions or feelings as long as tasks are completed and goals are reached.

There's a downside to this style: people who continually practice it are often intimidating. They tend to demand blind obedience, practice one-way communication, and act controlling and negative. What they want done is usually accomplished quickly and in the way they want it. But their method can result in resentment among followers, a climate of fear, and high turnover.

There is a time and a place for the dominating style—one in which it is especially effective. It is often very useful during a crisis, which is one reason why the military uses it. In wartime, soldiers must be prepared to act immediately and with blind faith in their leader. Questioning things in that situation could be deadly.

Unfortunately, many people with limited leadership experience believe that domination is the "definition of leadership." In their minds, leading means giving orders; anything less will result in ineffectiveness or unwanted compromise. But that simply isn't true. Dwight D. Eisenhower, World War II General and later President of the United States said, "You do not lead by hitting people over the head — that's assault, not leadership."

2. THE NEGOTIATING LEADER

Let me begin by pointing out that some aspiring leaders are uncomfortable with the idea of negotiating. For them the term negotiation brings to mind unacceptable compromise, or giving up things that they don't want to lose. But an effective negotiating leader is not a loser; he's a winner who helps others win.

The successful negotiating leader desires to create a win-win-win in every situation. He wants to create wins for (1) the organization, (2) his followers, and (3) himself. To do that, he learns to judge what the organization needs, discern what his followers want, and communicate his own desires.

> *An effective negotiating leader is not a loser; he's a winner who helps others win.*

Here are nine principles that will enable you to lead successfully by negotiating:

A. **Recognize your goal is a win-win-win.** A leader will not succeed if his negotiations repeatedly produce losers as well as winners. Leaders who allow someone to lose can cause others to distrust and resent them. On the other hand, when the leader has a reputation for causing everyone to win, others are anxious to follow her leadership. And if she must make choices determining who wins first, the negotiating leader chooses in the following order: first the organization, then followers, and finally herself.

B. **Start negotiations with high expectations.** Your attitude at the beginning of a task determines its outcome more than any other factor. If you believe that you can produce a win-win-win, you probably can. If you don't believe it, you probably can't.

C. **Predetermine what will cause you to walk away from negotiations.** No negotiation should be continued "at all costs." Any time you believe that you cannot walk away from a negotiation, the likelihood of producing a win-lose situation increases dramatically.

To prevent that from happening, determine ahead of time what will cause you to break off negotiations. Here is my list. Use it to help you create yours:

a. Bad attitudes
b. Distrust
c. A winner-loser scenario
d. All give and no take
e. Threats
f. Secrets
g. Personal attacks or criticism
h. Closed-mindedness

D. Separate the people from the issues. Negotiations that focus on people rather than issues are destined either to break down or create losers as well as winners. Avoid letting personalities become the subject of negotiations. Focus on problems to be solved together instead.

E. Discover up front what the other person wants. Since your goal is to produce a situation where everyone wins, it's best to know what everyone wants. Take time to find out what the other person wants before you negotiate. It will make the task easier for everyone, and the negotiations will be much faster. Also communicate that all the issues need to be put on the table up front, not added as you go along. The negotiation process rarely results in "wins" for everyone when issues and wants keep getting added to the list.

An attitude that seeks multiple options enhances flexibility and the chances of success for everyone.

F. Generate a variety of options before deciding. One of the greatest strengths of a negotiating style is that it creates options and allows flexibility. Any time you approach a conflict with a set agenda and no willingness to explore options, the negotiation is liable to break down or create losers. On the other hand, an attitude that seeks multiple options enhances flexibility and the chances of success for everyone.

G. Don't match concessions one to one. Some negotiators, out of a desire to be fair, seek to match concessions one-for-one. They believe that if one person compromises on one point then the other should concede on one point. Now, if all points or issues were exactly equal, that might work. The problem is that they're not. One of your concessions might be the equivalent of eight for the other person. For that reason, avoid taking points from each side one at a time. Instead, try to build a winning situation for each person, granting what he must have in order to be a "winner" and including concessions with which he can live .

H. Carefully consider the ridiculous offer. Never automatically throw out any ridiculous offer you receive during a negotiation. Often, great opportunities can be found in what at first appears to be outrageous. Ridiculous offers often:

    a. Are things you've never thought of before
    b. Are outside of the normal structure
    c. Will take extra effort
    d. Seem too good to be true
    e. Will raise questions

Look for the benefits in any offer. You may find that they outweigh the disadvantages that were initially apparent.

I. Have a time limit and a tangible way to evaluate the deal. It's difficult for a negotiation to be successful until you define what success means for you. Determine what conditions will have to be met in order for everyone to know that you've "won," and set a time when you will make that judgement.

The negotiating style of leadership can be very effective, particularly when you are working with creative and flexible people. And it works especially well with people who are dedicated to the success of the organization.

3. THE PERSUADING STYLE

Sometimes a leader finds himself in a position where he believes he knows what is best for the organization and his followers, but they don't yet share his conviction. That's when the persuading style of leadership can be very effective. A persuading leader uses positive verbal appeals to produce within others a feeling similar to his.

Persuading others is more than just sharing your point of view. That alone won't convince anyone to change. In addition, it requires some other tools of persuasion. But like any type of leadership, these tools must be used with appropriate motives and attitude. Here are six principles of persuasion to use as guidelines:

1. Passion is foundational. You might remember that people are best persuaded by those who are themselves convinced. Passion, or the outward display of inward conviction, lays the groundwork for persuasion to take place.

2. Confidence is essential. When followers are confident in the leader, they're able to have confidence in the leader's ideas. Expressing your ideas with authority and confidence does wonders to encourage others to believe and follow you.

3. Discernment is critical. If you don't know where your people are (what they currently feel and believe about the issue), you can't lead them over to your side. Discernment notices the "You Are Here" sign over the heads of followers, and uses it to map out the path to a new point of view.

4. Reasons are evident. Once you know where the people are, you must give them good reasons to change. Different types of appeals were explained in Chapter Nine. The reasons you give will serve as arrows pointing followers in the direction you want them to go.

5. Integrity is fundamental. Aristotle spoke of three ingredients in persuasion: logos , which appeals to reason; pathos, which appeals to emotion; and ethos, which involves credibility. Followers must believe that you are who you say you are before you can influence them. Credibility makes the difference between a persuasive leader and a manipulative opportunist.

6. Love is motivational. Any time you desire to persuade others, you must make it clear to them that you have their best interests at heart. Remember this crucial truth: People don't care how much you know until they know how much you care.

The primary keys to persuasive leadership are vision, communication, and motivation. If you have a worthwhile vision for your organization and people, and can communicate that vision to others and motivate them to act on it, you can succeed.

4. THE MODELING LEADER

Modeling has a tremendous impact on people, as every parent certainly knows. What father or mother hasn't been startled when their preschooler begins using expressions the parents used repeatedly in front of them. With little children, we may be able to convince them to "do as I say, not as I do." But when they reach their teenage years, kids begin behaving as their parents do no matter what they have been told.

Even adults are strongly influenced by the modeling of others. When another person does something positive that we admire, and we can see how and why he did it, we naturally desire to follow and do the same. Positive example prompts positive action.

People who join you
are always more committed than those
who simply follow behind you.

Former United States vice president Hubert H. Humphrey said, "This, then, is the test we must set for ourselves; not to march alone but to march in such a way that others will wish to join us." People who join you are always more committed than those who simply follow behind you. And they will walk farther, too.

5. THE EMPOWERING LEADER

The highest form of leadership is empowerment, because it is a partnership in success. The empowering leader uses his relationships to connect with his people and communicate his vision to them. Then he motivates them to believe they can achieve it and equips them to accomplish it.

Pittacus, the ancient war hero and wise man, said, "The measure of a man is what he does with power." The average leader tends to make the preservation of power his primary concern. He hoards it because he sees it as a limited resource, something he cannot easily replace. He is equally reluctant to relinquish the privileges that power brings.

The empowering leader, on the other hand, takes the power he has and gives it away to his people. He trains and develops them to assume power and responsibility and then gives them authority. As a result, the people around him share in his success.

Empowering leaders have six characteristics that make them stand out:

1. They have a vision bigger than themselves. Leaders with a small vision have no reason to employ or empower others. The greater the vision, the greater the need for others to help make it a reality. The greatest leaders have a vision much larger than themselves and what they can do alone.

2. They believe in people. I have yet to see an empowering leader who did not believe in people. All of them genuinely like people and want to help and be helped by them. It's true that only when you believe that others can help you will they actually be able to help you.

3. They have an excellent self-image. One reason empowering leaders are able freely to share power with others is that they have an excellent self-image. They are aware of their own strengths and weaknesses and like who they are. So they're not threatened by the idea of being surpassed by the people they empower, which is always a possibility.

4. They are people developers. The desire to help others grow and improve is always at the heart of an empowering leader. He seeks to help others develop until they reach their potential, until they become great leaders in their own right. Ralph Nader said, "I start with the premise that the function of leadership is to produce more leaders, not more followers." Empowering leaders do exactly that by giving their time, money, and energy to others who desire to better themselves.

> *Those closest to the leader determine*
> *the success level of that leader.*

5. They have a servant's heart. Their willingness to share themselves shows that empowering leaders desire to serve their fellow men. They believe that the best way to improve their world is by helping others.

6. They are highly successful. Empowering leaders are a living example of what I consider one of the greatest of all leadership principles: Those closest to the leader determine the success level

of that leader. Because they work with and through others, empowering leaders' efforts are multiplied. And they are capable of achieving the greatest of success.

LEADERSHIP STYLE	REQUIREMENT	RESULT	POTENTIAL BREAKDOWN
Dominating	Blind obedience from followers	Immediate action	Causes negative reactions, high turnover
Negotiating	Mutual victory	Entrepreneurship	If one party does not perform, the other loses
Persuading	Ability to motivate others	Winning Attitudes	If motivator absent nothing happens
Modeling	Demonstrate tasks for followers	Loyalty and bondedness	If leader falls the followers suffer more harm
Empowering	Investment of time and resources	Extraordinary Success	Can become codependent

Effective leaders utilize all of the leadership styles at one time or another, but the greatest leaders make empowerment their goal. They know that since their ultimate success depends on other people, the best way to succeed is to help those people to become more effective. They share their resources, their power, and ultimately, their success.

Margaret Thatcher, former prime minister of England, said, "Being in power is like being a lady. If you have to tell people you are, you aren't." Likewise, if you have to tell the people around you that you're their leader, you aren't. Instead, develop your leadership skills and credibility with your people. Then in time, they will acknowledge you as their leader. Your influence will speak for itself.

One of the greatest business leaders in American history was Andrew Carnegie. A poor immigrant from Scotland, he developed a multimillion-dollar steel company at the turn of the century, and later established more than 2,500 libraries and many philanthropic institutions, such as the Carnegie Institute of Pittsburgh, the

Carnegie Institution at Washington, the Carnegie Foundation for the Advancement of Teaching, the Carnegie Endowment for International Peace, and the Carnegie Corporation of New York. It is estimated that by the time of his death in 1919, he had given away over $350 million.

Carnegie was known as a leader who recognized and developed other leaders. He surrounded himself with successful people, a practice for which he credited his success. He once said, "No man will make a great leader who wants to do it all himself, or to get all the credit for doing it." To further express his conviction, he requested the following inscription on his tombstone: "Here lies a man who knew how to enlist the service of better men than himself."

To become a great success
you must enlist others to help you. And to do
that, you must become a leader.

Just like Carnegie, if you want to be a successful person in this life, you cannot do it all by yourself. To become a great success, you must enlist others to help you. And to do that, you must become a leader. Once you do, achievement beyond your wildest dreams can become a reality. Becoming a leader is ultimately the greatest strategy for success.

SUCCESS STRATEGY ACTIVITIES

---

1. Take some time to create a leadership style journal for yourself. At the end of each day, recall each situation where you were required to lead others—employees, coworkers, family members, etc. Record the interaction in a sentence or two. Then, using the descriptions of each leadership style, determine which style you used in that interaction. At the end of a week, answer the following questions:

a. Which style did you use most often? (This often indicates your predominant leadership style.)

b. Is the style you used most often the most effective one for you? (NOTE: If you used the dominating style most often, you need to learn to use it only rarely.)

c. For each interaction, which style would have been most effective, the one you used, or a different style?

2. Learning to be a good model for others begins with picking a model to follow yourself. Pick at least two people you can use as role models. (Make at least one a person you know and spend some time with on a regular basis.) Make a list of the things you could learn from each role model, and write down what you can do to make the learning process more strategic.

3. Being a good leader means learning about leadership and growing on a continual basis. Write a personal plan for growth for yourself. List resources that you will use to promote growth, including books, articles, tapes, and conferences on leadership. The best plans tend to include at least a tape a week, a book a month, and a conference a year. If possible, find someone who is willing to grow along with you using the same or a similar plan. Sharing the growth will give you someone to discuss ideas with, help you maintain your enthusiasm, and keep you accountable to stay on your program.

4. Write down the names of the members of your immediate family. Next to each name, write down the person's primary interests, gifts, skills, and talents. Also write down their dream or vision for their life. (If you don't know it, sit down with each person and ask about it.) Then write briefly how you plan to help that person reach his potential. Your plan can involve teaching him, giving your time, assisting in projects, helping financially, finding him a mentor, etc. Begin implementing your plan immediately.

5. Make a complete list of the people outside of your family over whom you have influence. Then select the top 20 percent of those people to develop. Next to each of those top names, write down the person's primary interests, gifts, skills, and talents, and dreams. Also write down what you believe is that person's greatest poten-

tial, along with how you plan to help him reach it. Discuss your plans with the person to make sure that (1) he is willing and (2) your vision for him is consistent with his own. As soon as you have his approval, begin putting the plan into action.

———

AFTERWORD

Congratulations! If you have come this far you must be serious about your future. You want to be better; you want to impact others positively. If you have actually invested some time in the exercises, you are indeed hungry for change. One of my favorite expressions goes like this: "If you don't change directions, you'll end up where you're headed."

Perhaps you needed to be a more *positive* person. Maybe there is *failure* and disappointment in your past, and you need to put it in perspective and move on with confidence and faith. Is it *vision* you are lacking? First you must gather your own vision of your future, and next you need to learn to cast vision to others. *Goal setting* as well as *time* and *stress management* skills will be important allies as you move on in your journey.

Ultimately, it will be your ability to form *relationships* and connect with people, to *communicate* on all levels and to *motivate* others, and your decision to assume the role of *leadership* that will enable you to empower those you lead—the key to your success strategy.

Become a life-long student. My friend, Charlie "Tremendous" Jones, always says: "You will be the same five years from now as you are today except for two things – the people you meet and the books you read."

A few books that I would highly recommend are:

Developing the Leader Within You	John Maxwell
Developing the Leaders Around You	John Maxwell
The Success Journey	John Maxwell
Becoming a Person of Influence	Maxwell/Dornan
Make a Life, Not Just a Living	Ron Jensen
Over the Top	Zig Ziglar
Principled-Centered Leadership	Stephen Covey

On a personal note, your ultimate strategy for success is a belief that your life matters and that you have a specific purpose which no one else can fulfill. My personal goal is to always seek God's will for my life and then pursue it with passion and confidence. Any strategy for success that ignores faith and the spiritual, eternal considerations of life is not success at all.

You may not get out of life what you believe you deserve but you will typically get what you expect. Think big, love people, work hard with integrity, and trust God for the rewards. You will not be disappointed.
